ARE WE THERE YET?

One Sojourner's Journey through Dross Consumed and Gold Refined

Morgan Cheek

ISBN: 9780692126264

To Anonymous, known fully and completely by God alone.

TABLE OF CONTENTS

FOREWORD

I open my computer up and light a candle. It's one of those off-brand glass jars with the cheesy, seasonal sticker on the front. I take a sip of my coffee—always made into what a good friend deemed "Beyonce"-style (not super dark, not super light)—my current method of choice, almond milk creamer, flavored pumpkin spice. It's lukewarm. I put it in the microwave for 30 seconds. The door to the screened porch is open. It's mid-October and one of the first days that actually feels like fall. The crisp air and sound of nearby house finches is interrupted by a lawnmower, and, consequently, the sounds of neighboring barking dogs. I close the door. My phone beeps with a text from my mom. I should call her, I think. The coffee needs a few more seconds, and, as I stand by the microwave, my phone rings. It's the girls' school nurse. Ally has had two seizures since I dropped her off (it's now 8:30 AM). One of them looked different than usual. She seems okay now. What did I want them to do? I spill the coffee onto my open journal as I contemplate whether or not I should pick her up, knowing good and well she would most likely be fine the remainder of the day.

This, my friends, is just another day in the life of a mom with twins with special needs. In some ways, I have a feeling it's no different than yours. Things on the to-do list mixed with unexpected inter-ruptions and a few graces—some common, some unique—along the way. Zephaniah 2:3 says this:

> "Seek the Lord (search diligently for Him and regard Him as the foremost necessity of your life), all you humble of the land...seek humility (it as vital)."

(Amplified Version)

By the grace of God, for several years now, I can honestly say I have been diligently searching for the Lord. Sometimes He has been easier to find than others. I know He is here. I know that, as the next chapter of Zephaniah so clearly says, He is in our midst. Yet the humility thing gets me all tripped up. So often my pride seeps up in my mind and heart, and I begin to believe that what I want and what I think should be my current reality and are more pertinent than seeing who He is and what He's up to in the world around me. This current season of heart unrest has brought up a lot of doubts and questions in my mind. I would like to think that, as Eugene Peterson (2017) says, my life is a "lifelong practice of attending to the details of congru-ence—congruence between ends and means, congruence between what we do and the way we do it, congruence between what is written in Scripture and our living out what is written...congruence between preaching and living...congruence of the Word made flesh in Jesus with what is lived in our flesh." Sometimes it is. And sometimes? It's just not. Is that okay? Can I love Jesus—can I be a true follower of Christ—and spend moments, weeks, months, years struggling with authentic congruence?

I believe the answer to this is a resounding, reassuring *yes*.

This book is going to be full of simple yet profound moments from my days. I am going to be writing it in "real" time—a reality show book of sorts—because isn't that the stuff we crave? So often our pride gets in the way, and we want to share what we learned in the trenches after we have already cleaned up and walked out. We want to bandage up our wounds, give them a little time to heal, and then tell the war story. I'm writing this in the thick of the battle. Only God knows what the days ahead will hold—my obedience is going to be simply sharing. My prayer is that the Lord would give me a unique grace to have you, the reader, so deeply enter into the details of our story that you can practically feel our hearts beating simultaneously. After all, that's what all good stories do. I want to thank you in advance for the grace you are going to have to give me in order for this to happen. You are going to experience my flesh—a wrestling of sorts—in this story God has already written in our little family's life. The more we see someone's humanity, the more we see brokenness and mess. Yet, in ways only God Himself can make possible, this is also the route to experience true, deep community. As C. S. Lewis (2015) puts it, "Friendship is born at that moment when one person says to another: 'What! You too? I thought I was the only one.'" You, my friend, are not alone. We are all called to endure, and to do this, we must endure together. There is no other way. These pages are my small contribution to encouraging you to humbly live out the horribly beautiful journey the God of the universe has laid out for you. To Him be the glory.

INTRODUCTION

Tensions are always high in the midst of travel. You can sense it in an airport—the hustle and bustle, oftentimes impatience, of it all. It's as if we are all under mutual agreement that this "somewhere in the middle" is not where we are supposed to be. Adults (usually) are pretty subtle in the wait. Children have a way of simply telling it like it is. Even nonverbal children like our own cry and whine the longer they have to wait for the destination. The question, "Are we there yet?" can come up over and over and over. The irony of it all is that once we are "there," we begin thinking about the next target. Why is this? Why can't we simply enjoy the journey—what's so bad about the in-between? The truth is, I think that deep down we always feel like there is something better awaiting us. In some aspects, this is good because it lends itself to eyes with eternal lenses. C. S. Lewis (1960) words it this way:

"If we find ourselves with a desire that nothing in this world can satisfy, the most probable explanation is that we were made for another world."

To that, I would give a resounding amen. Yet, are we called to enjoy the sojourning? And if so, how?

This book is written from a place of soul discomfort. I am currently feeling uncomfortable in the world we live in, restless in my own skin, awkward with all that this broken place entails. Can you relate?

What's the point of it all? If, ultimately, we are meant to live forever in the Kingdom of God, worshipping the Lord of lords on His throne forever and ever, then what are we supposed to do in the meantime? Is this part purposeful? I believe God's Word is clear that the answer to that question is absolutely yes. What if the middle is not a means to an end but an intentional piece of what God is doing? Shouldn't that change the way we experience and live out our moments? I believe yes.

There is a hymn of old called, "How Firm a Foundation." This book is dedicated to its writer—someone who chose to remain anonymous, yet has impacted myself and others in hugely spiritual ways. The fourth stanza says this:

"When through fiery trials thy pathway shall lie, My grace, all sufficient, shall be thy supply; the flame shall not hurt thee; I only design Thy dross to consume, and thy gold to refine."

What if God is using all these moments—the seemingly big and seemingly small, the ones that appear easy and the ones that appear painstakingly hard, the days that feel mundane and the days that feel like Ebenezer stones—to consume that which is worthless and that which doesn't last in us in order to make Himself, who is purer than gold, shine through?

The chapters that follow are a conglomeration of learning to see God in all things and finding that joy seeps marvelously from a life lived out this way. It is a messy mix of both highs and lows of seeing God in everything and of desperately attempting to see Him in anything. My prayer for you is that as you read the details of our story— His story in our lives—you will see both the lavish love and grace of our Father and also the miracle of His presence in every single millisecond of each moment of every creature, human being, created thing on this planet. I long to fully experience life—to capture God Himself—in every circumstance and every person (all made in the image of God!) that I come in contact with today, tomorrow, and the next. I pray that for you too. Thanks for seeking His presence through the mustered-up words of this sinner made saint by His indescribable grace found in Jesus. May it be found—may He be found—in ways that only He could make possible. Onward and upward we go!

1

THESE FEEBLE HANDS

She bites her hand—always the left. It is beginning to scar... this feeble hand. She arches her back, throwing her head backward onto the back of the bath seat. She kicks her legs with no particular intention except rhythm, over and over. The water runs lukewarm. I squirt out some shampoo into my own left hand. I begin to sweat both from physical exertion and emotional frustration. Sometimes the internal turmoil hits so deep that I can feel it on the surface. It is a deeper hurt than I know how to articulate that I have watched my Bailey Grace do this *every single day* for over a thousand days. They say put one foot in front of the other—but what do you do when putting the next foot down is the thing that scares you the most?

Growing up in the buckle of the Bible belt (yes, this is a thing), there were many parts of Christianity that felt cheesy to me. It seemed like the more people were involved in the church, the less real they became to me.

"You become. It takes a long time. That's why it doesn't happen often to people who break easily, or have sharp edges, or who have to be carefully kept. Generally, by the time you are real, most of your hair has been loved off, and your eyes drop out and you get loose in the joints and very shabby. But these things don't matter at all, because once you are real you can't be ugly, except to people who don't understand" (*The Velveteen Rabbit*).

When I look at the stories of Scripture, I don't see a bunch of people putting on their Sunday best and robotically spouting out all the right answers. I see real human beings, in the midst of all their mess (and some of them were in a lot of mess!) being fiercely loved by God. I see God handpicking them out and, like a threshing tool, molding and pruning and turning regular, everyday people like you and me into vessels of the Living God.

But to do this?

They had to recognize their own feeble hands. They had to take off the mask of the false self (Brennan Manning) and stop pretending that the broken pieces weren't there.

> "Let the peace of Christ (the inner calm of one who walks daily with Him) be the controlling factor in your hearts (deciding and settling questions that arise). To this peace indeed you were called…"

> (Col. 3:15a, Amplified Bible)

I dry off my hands as best I can and count to three in a high-pitched voice. Am I counting for her or for me? I pick her up and wrap her up tight in the towel lying on the tile floor. As I dry her off, the arching and biting pick up a bit. I take a deep breath and smile down at the gorgeous threshing tool lying on the floor below. She smiles back in between motions. I continue to smile, and as I do, I whisper, "Sweet girl, it's all so beautiful, except for people who don't understand."

In this world we will have trouble, yet take heart, He has overcome the world (John 16:33).

2

THE LAME

Around the time the girls were first beginning to show signs of "something's not right" and "this is not normal," I began to pray fervently for healing. For over six months, I prayed desperately that God would heal our girls. What I meant by this I'm not quite sure. I guess I desired earthly fixing of the girls' brains, bodies, and lungs. I had heard of the miracles. I had read many instances of God answering yes to these prayers of desperation. I wanted ours.

> "Behold, at that time I am going to deal with all your oppressors; I will save the lame and gather the scattered, and I will turn their shame into praise and renown in every land where they have suffered."
>
> (Zeph. 3:19)

Jesus spent a lot of time with the crippled. While on earth, He was very drawn to those the world considered weak and lame. When our girls were first diagnosed, I always saw verses like the above and thought of them. It comforted me as a mom to think of Jesus rescuing the girls from all they have suffered from and bringing them into His Kingdom.

No more seizures.
No more inability to fully communicate.
No more unexplainable hurting and crying and pain.

Before we got our diagnosis, I got a call that the last big genetics test had come back lacking. There was not going to be any hope for answers—at least not in the near future. This very same day is the day that I felt my heart stir to stop praying for earthly healing. I can't explain it, really; I'm not sure why. I just know that, in those moments, God's Spirit in me released me to stop seeking earthly answers or changes. This is when freedom (and acceptance) began.

> "Likewise, the Spirit helps us in our weakness. For we do not know what to pray for as we ought, but the Spirit Himself intercedes for us with groanings too deep for words. And He who searches hearts knows what is the mind of the Spirit, because the Spirit intercedes for the saints according to the will of God."

(Rom. 8:26–27)

Groanings too deep for words. These days, this is how I would describe my prayers for Bailey Grace and Ally. Most days, I don't really know how to pray anymore. It has been years now of changing epilepsy patterns, respiratory illness turned days and nights of suffering into hospital stays, years of unexplainable crying out and pain and vomiting and unanswerable questions for two precious little pieces of my heart that I carry from place to place each and every day. And, in a very real and raw and processed way, I do not know what is worse: years and years more of this or the end of it. Unless you have walked through deep suffering with a child, these things are inexpressible—groans too deep for words. But God: He knows. He who ordained His Son to walk the streets of this broken world. He who decisively determined to have His Son persecuted, struck down, and crucified—He knows.

So what does this mean? This means that while I am fully convinced He is immeasurably able to bring about earthly healing for Ally and Bailey Grace, I am equally decided that, for at least today, His glory and their good is being produced through the "not yet." How? Why? This I do not know. But sometimes, in the midst of all we cannot, will not, aren't supposed to know, we must cling to that which we do. I know my God liberally supplies all that we need (Phil. 4:19). Whatever we do not have in this moment is that which we do not need. Whatever we do have in this moment is that which can't be taken away from us. Oh, that I would believe this for our girls. Dear reader, may your heart believe this for those you know (maybe yourself) in the midst of chronic, daily, seems-like-it-will-never-end suffering. Oh, but it will end! Behold, at that time He will display what has already been accomplished for you and for me at the cross. Today, Ally and Bailey Grace must not need fully functioning brains or bodies to be the Image Bearers they have been called to be. Today, it must not be required of them to be seizure-free for their ultimate good. Do I understand this? No. Do I have to? Absolutely not. His thoughts are not my thoughts. His ways are not my ways (Isa. 55:8). I do not have to understand it to believe it; I simply must know the One who fathoms, plans, and purposes all. He delights in practicing steadfast love, justice, and righteousness in the earth (Jer. 9:24).

The truth is, we are all disabled. We are unable to stay on the path. We get distracted by things that are not only temporal but also futile. Ally and Bailey Grace's ministry is massive. I don't just mean numbers; I mean their influence is one that would have never happened if my "natural" prayers for health would have been answered with a yes. I thank God—some days with clinched teeth—that He gave them the holy privilege of this suffering in their earthly bodies. Do I long for the day that they are healed and made whole? Of course. Yet, just like anyone who knows Jesus prays for his or her children, I desire God to accomplish all that He knows is best through their human lives. We all are simply vessels. Our bodies are perishable, and regardless of what you believe about eternity, everyone knows good and well that these jars of clay have expiration dates. Oh, that we would have eyes to see and ears to hear the glorious truth of the gospel of Jesus Christ! May we acknowledge—not just with our lips but also with our hearts—that there is much more to life than mere physical health. May we begin to have heavenly lenses that see our own disabilities, and may we praise Him all the more for the promise that Jesus's death and resurrection displayed all wrongs made right for all eternity. Groan away, Beloved; His hands are strong to hold.

3

HIS WORKMANSHIP

One of the glorious things about preschool is that Ally and Bailey Grace bring home artwork almost daily. For the first year, I treasured each and every piece and would store it away in a huge bin called "Preschool Memories." For the first time ever, when I received artwork last Friday, I made sure the girls weren't looking, and I did something I thought I never would: I threw it away. This time last year, I would have never done such a thing. I would have kept it stashed away in storage, ready to be looked at with pride if the moment ever hit. If I'm honest, a subconscious thought I have had is that if they were no longer with us, would I have wished I would have saved this square-shaped house? So why did I throw these particular pictures away? Let me explain. It occurred to me at the beginning of this school year that while the crafts might have "Ally" and "Bailey Grace" written perfectly at the bottom, these pictures and paintings were not my girls' doing. Sure, there was most likely a lot of hand-over-hand help, but at the end of the day, I knew in my heart that this was really the artwork of our attentive and patient classroom helpers. If I had opened their teal folders and a note saying "Done completely by Bailey Grace" was attached to a piece of white construction paper with a tiny yellow crayon marking, you can bet that masterpiece would have gone on the fridge. Why? Because it was hers. It would be authentically, completely hers.

> "For we are His workmanship, created in Christ Jesus
> for good works, which God prepared beforehand, that
> we should walk in them."

(Eph. 2:10)

This is how God sees you, you know. He is not expecting some Mozart, canvased, picture-perfect work to show up—nor does He want that. He wants you. God would rather have one act of goodness flowing out of a heart of love than ten counterfeit, going-through-the-motions activities, distant from authenticity all together. So, often, I set the bar really high for myself, forgetting that the bar has nothing to do with me at all. The truth is, Christ is the bar. He accomplished all I needed to be done in order for me to be in relationship with Him. He is the One in whom we are created! God has prepared the way; we simply have to take His hand and keep ours open. Only He can perform the beautiful work of the opening and clinging simultaneously. We so often get it backward, don't we? We cling to the things of this world while keeping open hands, minds, and hearts to the things of God. I so want to be the woman who has it all together. I want my lines cut perfectly straight, my letters scribbled like calligraphy, and my paints exactly in the lines. But God: He knows me better than I know myself. And He knows when I'm attempting to be something, to be someone, that I'm not. The beauty of it is that He doesn't want that false version of me that's really an attempt to be someone else. He wants me—asymmetrical lines and all. When He sees me, He sees His Son. Because of Christ, I am both already and simultaneously being made into the image of the One true God. The victory has been won. Beloved, I want to urge you, and to urge me, to come to the Father with our true selves. We are His workmanship, created in Christ Jesus for the works that only He knows.

His plans for us are good.
His purposes are sure.
He is our magnificent Creator, and we are His.

"You are the light of the world. A city set on a hill cannot be hidden. Nor do people light a lamp and put it under a basket, but on a stand, and it gives light to all the house. In the same way, let your light shine before others, so that they may see your good works and give glory to your Father who is in heaven."

(Matt. 5:14–16)

4

RAVE, NOT RANT

O nly a few chapters in, and I have already had to erase several
chapters of this fairly short book. It's a fine line, you know.
There seems to be a lot of gray in the business of glorifying
God and standing up for Jesus and simply ranting about the fallen
nature of man. We see it all the time—social media being a prime
medium. I would like to think most of us really want to represent
Christ well. We desire to see His name glorified. The problem is, our
flesh has different ideas altogether.

"While he (Jesus) was till speaking, Judas came, one
of the twelve, and with him a great crowd with swords
and clubs, from the chief priests and the elders of the
people. Now the betrayer had given them a sign, saying, 'The one I will kiss is the man; seize him.' And he
came up to Jesus at once and said, 'Greetings, Rabbi!'
And he kissed him. Jesus said to him, 'Friend, do what
you came to do.' Then they came up and laid hands
on Jesus and seized him. And behold, one of those
who were with Jesus stretched out his hand and drew
his sword and cut off his ear. Then Jesus said to him,

'Put your sword back into its place. For all who take
the sword will perish by the sword. Do you think that I
cannot appeal to my Father, and He will at once send
me more than twelve legions of angels? But how then
should the Scriptures be fulfilled, that it must be so?'"

(Matt. 26:47–54)

I love this story because it shows, so deeply, the state of humanity.
The disciples with Jesus had fallen asleep while Jesus was praying for
strength to do the very thing that would save them—save us—for all
eternity. Jesus calls Judas as friend, knowing good and well that Judas
is greeting him in order to betray him. It is recorded in John 18 that
"one of those who were with Jesus" was Peter. I'm not sure if Peter is
simply panicking or trying to be a good friend to Jesus, but either
way, Jesus's response makes it clear that he feels absolutely no need
to fight back; after all, this is what He came to do. It says in Luke 22
that Jesus actually touched the man's ear and healed it—the same
soldier who was seizing him to be taken to be crucified. To add to the
not-so-ironic irony, Peter denies friendship with Jesus a mere fifteen
verses later. Now, if Jesus was fully man and not fully God (which
He was both, by the way), and if He had lived in modern times, He
might have tweeted, "Thanks for having my back, bro" as a shout-out
to Peter. Yet, Jesus's very nature—the exact representation of God
Almighty—was love. And it was for love that He responded in all the
ways that He did.

I think we have a lot to learn from this.

What is your typical response when someone betrays you or someone
you love? How do you react on social media when someone expresses
a different opinion than yours? What emotions rise up whenever you
see someone making different social choices than you or living out
different theology than your own? If you are like me—so often I live

by reaction. Sure, I start out the day with God's Word open. I pray for the ability to be transformed. I ask the Spirit to lead my moments. Yet distraction, circumstance, and interruption set in, and suddenly I am cutting someone's ear off. We may be quick to recognize (and even repent of!) this tendency in ourselves, but do we offer grace when we see it in others? How do we resist the temptation to slander, lash out, rant at the broken world around us?

> "I will bless the Lord at all times; His praise shall continually be in my mouth. My soul makes its boast in the Lord; let the humble hear and be glad. Oh, magnify the Lord with me, and let us exalt His name together!"
>
> (Ps. 34:1–3)

> Defined by the praise that comes from our mouths.
> Magnifying the Lord and exalting His name together.
> Raving about God's goodness rather than ranting
> about the sin around and within.

How refreshing would this be? What if we spent time truly looking for the lovely—the image of God—in those around us, even those who carry stark differences from us?

> "So God created man in His own image, in the image of God He created Him; male and female He created them."
>
> (Gen. 1:27)

We are all created in the image of God. While sin may be oh so present, there is a reflection of the Almighty Himself in each and every person in each and every nation. If you have breath in your lungs and a heart that is beating, this is true of you.

> "Woe to him who quarrels with His Maker...shall the
> clay say to the potter, 'What are you doing?'"

> (pieces of Isa. 45:9, *The Message*)

I know. We are all super messy. And many times, the clay just appears to be a repulsive little lump of mud, merely in the way. Sometimes, it even seems as if the clay is an obstacle in the way of the Potter Himself. Yet who are we, who am I, to determine what the God over all the universe is up to? Friends, we don't know why God allows some of the choices and actions that He does. But may we never forget that He is sovereignly working good out of every single stinking thing. (And some of them seem to stink more than others!) Nothing and no one is worthless in His holy hands.

> "Now there are also many other things that Jesus did.
> Were every one of them to be written, I suppose that
> the world itself could not contain the books that would
> be written."

> (John 21:25)

Friends, His goodness is too high, too deep, too wide to see. His work is too numerable to name. Even so, let's try. Let's spend our moments calling out the good, calling out the God, in those around us. Let's continually have His praise on our lips—the praise of the One who knows no slander, no hate, no evil. May we rave and rave and rave some more about the One who has brought beauty from ashes and praise from mourning. Worthy, worthy, worthy. Holy, holy, holy. Faithful and true. Name it. Claim it. Praise it.

5

THE GIFT OF A MOMENT

"So teach us to number our days that we may get a heart of wisdom."

(Ps. 90:12)

It was a crisp autumn day, the kind where the air is finally cool enough to not smother you but just fresh enough to feel like a splash of cold water hitting your face as the wind blows. The leaves had not quite turned yet. It was the spring of fall.

I pushed the girls up and down a few hills, out of breath, yet determined to get to our secret spot. Every now and then, the adaptive stroller would hit a fallen leaf...*crunch, crunch, crunch.* We reached our destination, just under the pines. The sun hit it just so—in a way where we could feel its warmth, yet not be blinded by its light.

I got the girls out of the stroller and laid them down on a blanket, leaving a spot for me, right in the middle. As I lay between them, Ally squealed with delight as Bailey Grace kick, kick, kicked her legs. The pines blew with the breeze, and a crow let out his "Caa, caa, caa."

The gift of a moment.

The clock reads 5:46 AM. I open my Bible, inhaling and then exhaling deeply, and take a quick glance at the monitor. Beady eyes. It's Ally. Is she seizing? After watching a couple of seconds longer and seeing her arms loosely moving to the side, I determine no. She has 45 minutes until I will get her up for school—just enough time to get some more solid sleep. I go upstairs, being as quiet as possible so as not to wake up Bailey Grace. It doesn't work. Both girls smile at me as I walk in. I feel Ally's diaper; it's soaked full. Nothing has wet through the sheets, so thankfully nothing will need to be changed. I get her cleaned up, lift her back up on the pillow, brush her hair out of her face, and tuck her in tight. She closes her eyes immediately. I go over to Bailey Grace, who hasn't made a peep at this point. I check her diaper as well: dry. I flip her pillow to the cooler side, kiss her forehead, and pull her sheets back up. She's already back to sleep. I walk downstairs and sit right back down where I was, my Bible still open.

The gift of a moment.

I head to walk over to the stove and then turn around and turn on the television. Ally and Bailey Grace are secure in their highchairs, the ones that are made for infants and young toddlers yet still miraculously fit our ever-growing daughters. PJ Masks is on, one of the girls' favorites. With the colors, the constant activity, and the music, their eyes light up, and their hands begin to rhythmically move, communicating to me that they are loving their current situation. I walk back toward the kitchen area, open the freezer, and reach in to find some frozen veggies. Tonight is a chicken sausage bowl kind of night. It's a staple in our home and is not only cheap but also relatively healthy and filling. And easy. It's not unique to moms of kids with special needs that weeknight dinnertime is less about gourmet cooking and more about making sure everyone is fed and ready for bed at a decent hour. (Let's face it; this is every mom with young kids!) Hugh has already called, letting me know he is on the way home. I put the vegetables in the pan, letting them cook in some olive oil and spices as I get the chicken sausage out and place it in another skillet. I find some minute quinoa in the freezer and place it in a bowl, ready to be put in the microwave whenever I hear Hugh's car pull up. I then begin to feed the girls dinner—Stage 1 sweet potato baby-food pouches with yogurt for dessert, followed by a bolus for nutrition. There are days where eating by mouth is hard for Ally and Bailey Grace. Whether it's oncoming congestion, subconscious seizure activity, or gastric discomfort, we keep a towel around for the times that gagging pans out as food all over the chair and floor. Tonight, both girls welcome each and every bite of food and eat without a problem. Periodically, I walk over to the stove and stir. I am just starting to draw up the girls' nightly medications when I hear Hugh's truck pulling in to the driveway. I press "start" on the microwave. The girls can hear the door open, and I cry out (like every night), "It's Daddy!" They kick and laugh and wear smiles as big as Texas as he says hello (then quickly goes to change out of his germ-infected pediatrician attire). I plate Hugh's meal, and mine and as the girls finish their bolus feeds, we sit down and talk about the day.

The gift of a moment.

"For God so loved the world that He gave."

(John 3:16a)

The only thing keeping Him from falling to the ground are the nails hammered into His bloody limbs. He hangs, naked outside of a crown of thorns pounded relentlessly into His head. There is a sign reading, "This is the King of the Jews" hanging above. Soldiers and civilians alike mocked him, not only not caring about His pain but also finding satisfaction in it. The agony went on, Jesus not saying a word, even in the midst of doubts and sneers flying His way as His blood poured out below.

> "And when the sixth hour had come, there was darkness over the whole land until the ninth hour. And at the ninth hour Jesus cried with a loud voice, 'Eloi, Eloi, lema sabachthani?' which means, 'My God, my God, why have you forsaken me?'...and Jesus uttered a loud cry and breathed his last. And the curtain of the temple was torn in two, from top to bottom. And when the centurion, who stood facing Him, saw that in this way He breathed His last, he said, 'Truly, this man was the son of God!'"

(Mark 15:33–34, 37–39)

The gift of a moment.

17

6

HINDSIGHT

"Moses said, 'Please show me your glory.' And He said, 'I will make all my goodness pass before you, and will proclaim before you my name, 'The Lord.' And I will be gracious to whom I will be gracious, and will show mercy on whom I will show mercy. But,' he said, 'you cannot see my face, for man shall not see me and live.' And the Lord said, 'Behold, there is a place by me where you shall stand on the rock, and while my glory passes by I will put you in a cleft of the rock, and I will cover you with my hand until I have passed by. Then I will take away my hand, and you shall see my back, but my face shall not be seen.'"

(Exod. 33:18–23)

It seemed like a reasonable request. Moses was in the process of being God's mouthpiece to a stiff-necked people—a people who were seeing but not perceiving, hearing but not understanding. Moses, a self-proclaimed bad spokesman, simply wanted to see the face of the One he was representing. He wasn't asking for material things; he didn't want extra favor. He just wanted to see the face of God.

I remember.

I remember sitting in my living room, Googling disease after disease. We were in the process of waiting on several genetics tests to come back, and as I looked up many of the diagnoses, one thing was clear: whatever was going on was not "just hypotonia"—hypotonia (low muscle tone), the first symptom that was recognized as "something wrong" with our baby girls. Hypotonia is associated with hundreds of diseases with varying characteristics. I recall looking up YouTube videos for a particular disorder—one that required six weeks for the testing to come back—in which family after family told the story of their child and the life they had lived. I say lived because each and every one had passed away within months or very few years. It physically took my breath away as I tried to digest the reality that I could lose my baby daughters in a matter of days.

I remember.

I remember two long years later, finding out that we didn't have any of those diagnoses after all. We had HECW2, which I have nervously joked when asked what it is, "Who the hec(k) knows?" This disease in which I very well could be putting up a similar YouTube video or not—this disease that supposedly would, will, does affect our girls' brains, hearts, and lungs. This disease that is so unknown it comes with no prognosis or detail. For over two years, I longed for answers—if only I had known that our answer was going to come with more questions than not. I remember sitting in the genetics office and being told that while no one knew exactly what to expect, the expectation was that this disease would shorten our girls' lives to a significant extent. Regardless, albeit a miracle, they were not going to live independent lives. They most likely would not live seizure-free lives. We would always need to be cautious of the next bad illness. I got into my car and simply asked God, "What now?"

I remember.

I remember Hugh and me confidently determining he was called to go to Peru for a week. It was mid-January, and within one day of his absence, both girls were fighting horrific colds. We were at my parents' house in Tennessee, and snow had recently fallen on the ground. After being up with them all night, two nights in a row, I looked outside to the ground and saw the sun coming up, the leftover bits of snow glistening like diamonds. I had not yet talked to Hugh, as his phone service was minimal, but as I looked over at Ally and realized she wasn't strong enough to "get up for the day," I knew we were headed to Children's. As my mom drove me and the girls back to Birmingham, both girls coughing and vomiting mucus the entire way, I didn't have time to do my typical processing. One night at the hospital with Ally turned into two more nights at the hospital with Bailey Grace. When Hugh got home at the end of the week, I felt like we had survived a battle. The girls had never been in the hospital simultaneously, and they have not been in the hospital at the same time since.

I actually have a horrible memory. Call it stress, lack of sleep, or merely scattered, there are many parts and pieces of the past four years I can't recall. There are several, however—both easy and hard—that come to mind quickly. However blurry and fuzzy some of the details are, one thing is crystal clear. From the very first time I saw the girls in my womb to this very morning in which I fed them their stage 1 baby food for breakfast, I may have specific details that come to mind, but in all of them, it's God's presence—Immanuel—I remember the most. You see, the miraculous thing is not that we have walked through all we have and survived (although some days this feels like a feat!). The miracle in it all is that regardless of my faith or lack thereof, He was right there with us—completely in the thick of it. He quite literally has been near in the darkest, most challenging moments of our days.

When I look back on these times, I don't feel a deep sickness in the pit of my stomach. I have fond, comforting memories of God holding tightly onto me and giving me wisdom, discernment, endurance, and peace in the midst of what the world would tell me is a nightmare. As I read Exodus 33, I am reminded that in order to give us the holy privilege of seeing His glory, He often covers us with His hand. When His hand is upon us, it might seem dark, yet it is this very darkness that shows us He's all the more closer, not farther. In hindsight, we will always see His back. We can always look back and see His ever-steadfast, ever-faithful Presence with us in all things. This changes everything, including how we interpret what is going on with us in the here and now. We are in the middle of some blah days. Both girls are having unpredictable seizure patterns, and as a mom, it's beyond frustrating to watch helplessly as their brains malfunction. As I look back on all He has done in the past, though, I am spurred on to hope in what He is doing in the here and now—even as it doesn't make sense from my vantage point. We may not know what He is doing in these moments, but we can rest assure that He is intentional, active, and present.

So what about you?

Think back on some times when you've seen His back, that, in hindsight, it was obvious He was doing much more than you could have possibly known at the time. The same God who is encouraging my heart and giving me endurance is the One who longs to do the same for you. Is it dark? Don't worry, beloved, it is just His holy hand, and His arm is never too short.

Remember, and take hold of His faithfulness.
Remember, and recognize His goodness.
Remember, and see His never-changing hold.
Remember.

7

FAMILY DINNER

I made a roast. Well, actually, I technically made the roast the day before. There I was, doing some yoga after folding laundry before picking up the girls from school, when it hit me. It was small group night. Not only did I not need to have the Crock-Pot on but also needed to pick up some cookies to bring to share. So here we were, Wednesday, with a roast and potatoes ready to heat up.

Wednesdays are the days the girls don't go to school. Our dear friend Stephanie, who is really like family, has been coming on Wednesday afternoons since the girls were four months old. Week after week after week, she does physical therapy with the girls while I sit and chat or get things done around the house—whichever seems like the priority that day. I had spent the morning pushing the girls around the neighborhood in their somewhat new adaptive stroller, and the autumn air had me feeling all kinds of contentment.

Back to the roast.

There isn't a week that passes when I don't have at least a moment of wishing that we could have family dinners. Every so often, we sit around the table as Hugh and I eat dinner and the girls get their bolus feeds. Most of the time, the witching hour and the stagnant nature of tube feeding requires more entertainment than simple conversation;

so, often, we sit in front of the television as the girls watch Disney. On this particular night, Hugh and I ate the somewhat leftover roast as Puppy Dog Pals played in the background. We gave the girls their medications, brushed their teeth, read a book, and then carried them up the stairs to their room. My arms and legs were already tired from a day full of carrying 40 pounds, twice over, everywhere throughout the day. Suddenly, for reasons I cannot explain, my soul felt heavier than my daughters' bodies did.

We said a prayer, cleaned the girls' tube sites, changed their diapers, and then put them in bed. Hugh and I went downstairs and had the same conversation we have almost every night: television or reading? We decided it was a television night, and as we watched an episode of one of our favorite shows, we waited on Bailey Grace (and maybe Ally) to have one, two, maybe three seizures. I would glance down every few seconds, and as soon as I saw beady eyes light up on the monitor screen (signaling Bailey Grace was awake and seizing), Hugh went upstairs. We tend to switch out on who goes in. We used to both always go, yet the pain of watching the seizures over and over and over again felt too much. Somehow, watching behind the screen seemed easier—at least every other time.

After about three minutes (a somewhat shorter event), Hugh came back down, and we restarted the show. We sat in silence for a few minutes, and as the television went to a commercial break, I simply said, "I'm so sick of watching seizures."

"I know," Hugh responded.

But that wasn't enough.

Suddenly, the anger from the strain of the day, month, year, life came bubbling out.

"*Do* you know?" I sputtered. "I do this all day every day. This is my life. I don't know any other mom who has two kids who suffer as much as ours. As if it was not enough that Bailey Grace's seizures don't stop, we had to add Ally to the mix. It's just ridiculous, really."

Now, any of you who are married know the drill. When one spouse gets angry—maybe at the other, maybe for random uncontrolled circumstances—most of the time, the other gets defensive. When the other gets defensive, very often, spouse number one gets angrier. So there we were, me venting frustrations with seizures. The next thing we know, we are debating whether or not the average family gets out of their house more than we do. I wish I were kidding, and even typing this makes me see the silliness of it all.

In our hurt, why is it tempting to push people away instead of drawing them near? Why does it seem easier to isolate ourselves in pain instead of reaching out?

> "He gives power to the faint, and to him who has no might he increases strength. Even youths shall faint and be weary, and young men shall fall exhausted; but they who wait for the Lord shall renew their strength; they shall mount up with wings like eagles; they shall run and not be weary; they shall walk and not faint."

> (Isa. 40:29–31)

Hugh eventually turned off the television. He ground some coffee beans for the morning as I started the dishwasher and laid out some of the medical supplies for the next day. We went to the bathroom, brushed our teeth, turned off the light, and got in bed in silence.

"I love you," Hugh whispered.

"I love you too," I whispered back, a tear beginning to well up in my eye and stream down my face. Sometimes tears shed in the dark feel safer.

"I'm sorry I was angry," I cracked out.

"It's okay. I'm sorry I didn't know how to love you in that moment," Hugh responded.

We were quiet for a few minutes until Hugh broke the silence with this: "Hey, Mo, I love our life. I think we have a lot of fun."

I smiled.

"I love our life too, babe—whether we get out of the house more than 50 percent of the people we know in the world or not. I like it here."

I meant it.

We kissed goodnight, and both drifted off to sleep, not sure when the first little girl would wake up crying, signaling she needed us.

"He will not allow your foot to slip; He who keeps you will not slumber."

(Ps. 121:3)

After a couple of middle-of-the-night wake-ups, the alarm went off. It was 5:30 AM, and being a morning person, I jumped right up. I was ready to begin the day again, whatever the day held. He gives strength. Oh, how He gives.

8

THREE YEARS

I recently started getting photo flashbacks on my phone. I love it, and it is always such a good reminder for God's provision in our lives—the hindsight, if you will. The app will often pull up both last year and the year before. Yesterday, as I scrolled through the memories, they were eerily similar.

October 20, 2015:
I remember it like it was yesterday. It was a sweet season of life, marked deeply with medical community. Hugh was in residency, working upwards 80 hours a week. The twins had just been given a loose diagnosis of HECW2. We held a small group Bible study at our house for residents and their significant others, often having the girls meet on one side of the house and the guys on the other. It was a small space, yet somehow seemed to work. Most of these precious people had been a part of this process with us from the beginning. While residents, many of them were training in pediatrics. I will never forget the first moment I looked down at the monitor and realized something strange was going on. Early on, the girls had a lot of issues with nighttime vomiting. Some of it related to gastroparesis, some of it acid reflux, some of it (we now believe) to be epileptic activity. On this particular small group night, I glanced down to see Bailey Grace, seemingly wide awake. I jumped up, assuming I might catch things before the mess began, yet I paused

at the bottom of the staircase. I had never seen a seizure in my life, but something told me that she was having one. Nevertheless, I didn't panic. I didn't run up the stairs. It was as if I knew that as soon as I saw what I inevitably would, we would be entering into a new season of this disease. As I got next to her crib, it was obvious. I called for Hugh, and he confirmed what I already knew to be true. I will never know why I never once panicked during those early seizure days—God's grace my only assumption. A pattern began that night that hasn't ended since. Two very short nights later, while sitting next to Bailey Grace as she seized, we looked over at Ally as she began to tremor as well. I was both shocked and not surprised all in the same breath.

October 25, 2016:
It was the girls first Halloween week at preschool. I was beyond excited for them to begin to make some school memories. Thursday was Halloween dress-up day. This was the first year that they had the wheelchairs during Halloween; and Hugh and I (along with some serious Pinterest help) had worked hard to ensure their costumes were impressive. Ally was a ladybug, her wings attached to her wheelchair; Bailey Grace was a bumblebee, a golden hive enveloping the chair she sat in. On Tuesday, it was pretty clear that we were not going to make it to the party. Between the two of them, Ally was struggling to breathe comfortably, and before we knew it, we were back at Children's. The costumes, while we were able to wear them a few days later, stayed tucked away in the garage. My heart hurt. It might have been a silly secular holiday, but it represented carefree fun and community in my mind. I felt so sad for the girls that after all they had been through already, they were missing out on a celebration.

October 21, 2017:
I look through the flashbacks for the past couple of years, and one thing is clear: this doesn't tend to be an easy week for our family. I spend the next day or so looking into every single sign: are we having more seizures than usual? Do those sneezes mean something?

Did the spots of blood I just vented up warrant a doctor's call? What will this year hold?

I want to tell you that I always trust what God is doing. I would like you to think that my faith doesn't waver. But the truth? The truth is that so often, I begin the slippery game of assuming that God is going to teach us through the hard lesson. So many times, I'm convinced that severe mercies must be more effective than common graces. The reality? The only thing that's consistent about October 2015 and October 2016 is true for 2017 as well. God is sovereignly in control. He knows what He's doing. He's working for His glory and our good. He never fails. He never leaves us. His ways are perfect. He can always be trusted. These things trump anything else that might come out of His glorious plans—where are still to prosper—and give us hope and a future. While prospering may look differently than we expect, and maybe the story is going to take a few (a lot!) more turns than we anticipated, the reality that His control is a safe place for us has not and does not and will not change. He is always faithful. So today, I do not have to give way to the fear that this week is automatically going to be full of hard things. Instead, I can simply trust Him to be God. I can connect the dots of the years to His sovereign grace in my life instead of trying to figure out the lines in between. Why? Because God is God, and I am not, and that is a good, good thing. The truth is that the knowledge of the Holy One— knowledge that He knows—helps me to drive out the fear of needing to know all things. The reality is that if I knew what was always around the corner, wouldn't I be tempted to fear, anyway? Sure, there would be days and weeks and moments where I saw that life was going to be easy peasy and so I might sail through those times, but what about the hard stuff? What would awareness of the tribulation ahead benefit? Friends, I do not need to know what October 2018 carries—and you don't need to know what is up ahead either. May we, as Matthew 6:34 exhorts us, not worry about tomorrow, for each day has enough trouble for its own, and God is enough in all things. Three years. Three years of God's perfect plans playing out in His perfect way at His perfect time. This is our ultimate reality. To God be the glory!

9

LIGHT IN THE DARKNESS

I wake up, this time moving a little slower than usual. Last night was night number two of Bailey Grace being awake with unknown distress. Was she in pain? Was it her G-tube? Should we not have discontinued that medicine? Does her throat hurt? Is she getting sick? Is she having more seizures than usual? Either way, sleep has not been near to this home.

Yesterday was number eight. Yesterday, we found out for the eighth time in two years that birth parents we had prayed for and opened our hearts to say, 'Yes' to did not say, 'Yes' to us. This family in particular had shown great interest in us; they had asked us questions about the hospital stay, extended family, and what we would name the little boy who was growing in the birth mom's womb. Like every time before, we danced the tightrope of softening our hearts to what could be without fully jumping into the deep end to what might not. When I got the e-mail—the one that said they had in fact chosen another family—many of the truths that my soul knows to be true felt distant. Sometimes the reality of any given moment blurs us to the greater reality that's unseen. I spent the day fighting to believe the things I so desperately wanted to take root again in my heart.

I tried to remember all the promises I would tell a dear friend in the same situation: that God is for them. That He is sovereignly in control. That He knows best. That all His no's are simply leading to a greater, yes. That one day we will understand. It is easy to stand in confidence when we are running in the light, but what about when we are sitting in the dark?

I walked into the living room, pajamas still on, and went to unload the dishwasher as quietly as I could. I started to turn on a light but instead went to light a candle. This simple act carries a lot of meaning in my heart. The candle itself holds no weight, yet I often light a candle in the morning to remind myself that, "a bruised reed He will not break, and a smoldering wick he will not snuff out" (Isa. 42:3). So often, whether from the night's unpredictable events or whatever the new day holds, I wake up feeling bruised. I wonder if I can do it again yet another day (I can't). This morning, as I lit that same candle, I was reminded that the light was most easily seen in the dark. I glanced up at the window in front of me and saw the stars glimmering in the early-morning sky. It's always darkest before the dawn, you know. I went to turn on the kitchen light and quickly realized that the stars would no longer be visible to me if I did so. I stopped. I thought of Psalm 19:1:

> "The heavens declare the glory of God; and the sky
> above proclaims His handiwork."

The sky and these little lights gleaming up above, far beyond my comprehension, are the works of His hands.

The leaves that were beginning to change from green to beautiful hues of orange, red, and yellow—this was His doing.

All the flowers and animals and landscapes in all their detailed magnificence—His creation.

This God. This God whom I long to trust and worship and lean on fully—He is capable of all this and more. If He is able to do the miraculous things above, surely He is able to do more than I can ever comprehend. If He is the maker of these stars, surely He knows how to best do a work in my heart. And the darkness around just brings more focus to the light. The darker it is, the brighter the Light seems.

I stand by the window for a moment longer and stare intently at the stars above. I sit down on the couch, open my Bible, and look at the candle lit in front of me. The sides of the glass are beginning to look charred, yet the flame still burns. No matter how dark the room is, its light carries on. And, thanks be to God, so will I.

10

I MUST FOCUS ON HIS PROVISION

I have never been in a near-drowning situation, never felt the waters close up in my throat and fill my chest, never gasped and sputtered and tried to muster up just one more second of closed lips. I *have* been in two wrecks, both of which could have taken my earthly life. I remember the seconds before the initial crash. Each time, my natural reaction was to take a deep breath in and tense my body up, attempting to prepare for the unknown that was certainly going to occur. I have had this thought run through my mind in less than seconds: *Am I going to die? Is this going to be the way I end my exile on earth?* In some ways, I guess drowning and car collisions aren't too different, after all.

This morning, it felt a little bit like I was drowning.

I am no stranger to feeling as if I am suffocating in my own surroundings. I inhaled and exhaled as deeply as I knew how before sitting down to beg God yet again for soul nourishment. The truth is, my physical body was doing fine. Tired, yes, but otherwise fine. It was my soul that yearned for oxygen. They say oxygen is colorless and odorless. This thing—this element that has no smell and cannot be seen—is the very life-supporting component to anything and everything that occurs on this earth. Very often, I've feared silent aspiration for our girls. Because they choke, in some form, almost daily, I always wonder how protected their lungs actually could be. Almost every night, I wordlessly ask God to watch over them as they sleep and guard them from breathing into their little lungs something that doesn't belong. Do I pray as fervently for the silent aspiration of my soul? As I struggle to breathe in truth, I fear that I do not. The reality is, I have allowed things into my mind and heart in recent days that just didn't belong. I have spent minutes—no, hours—scrolling through a device that will never satisfy. I've had hurtful and ugly thoughts about those I claim to love that would cause my cheeks to beat hot red if ever I was found out. I've wondered if a different life would bring satisfaction and freedom that this one just doesn't seem to provide right now. I've lusted after new outfits and home décor and fine dining experiences that just might put a Band-Aid on the gaping open wound that feels like it's on its way to amputating my very soul. And, maybe worst of all, I have barely even fought the very emotions that were choking truth out of me. The love-hate relationship I have with sin is as real as the Spirit and flesh I contain. This is me, and while it's embarrassing and awkward to type out, it's as real as the mismatched socks I'm wearing on my always cold feet. Oh, I'm drowning all right.

As a follower of Christ, I find it very tempting to portray my sanctification as farther along than it truly is. It's always easier to share the first couple of layers and pretend the next don't exist. But God? He's not only not fooled but also is not surprised. He is all too aware of the darkness of our sinful nature. From the first moment that Eve took the bite of the fruit—the fruit that seemed like it would taste better than all the goodness in front of her—we have been biting into the lie that something outside of God and His plan for us would be better. So, instead of hiding the junk that's happening in my home and in my heart, I want to be upfront and tell you, as best I can, the good, the bad, and the ugly of wrestling to believe the promises of God. Because the reality is, in the midst of all the mess

I have typed above, God has still been faithful. He has been faithful to grant me grace in a handwritten letter of encouragement from a friend. He has been faithful to give Hugh and myself energy to care for our girls through the night in the middle of another unknown woe. He has been faithful to give me conversations with my sister that have been raw, precious, and healing. He has been faithful to show up in the sunshine on my face, the crisp air of the fall, and the friendship of the Body of Christ. I am not alone. He has truly been faithful to provide. Maybe that's the point. Maybe these trials—these necessary trials (1 Pet. 1:6)—are here to serve as catalysts for our minds and hearts. Like oxygen, while we can't physically see Him, we can experience the provision and love of God around and within us on a moment-by-moment basis. And when it seems as if we are struggling for the next breath, He's there to do the breathing for us. I must focus on His provision, or my soul dies. I must be desperate to see His presence and grace not after but smack-dab in the middle of my own brokenness. While we were yet sinners, Christ died for us (Rom. 5:8). It's that simple. In my wandering, He is behind and before. In my struggling, He is poised. In my emotional chaos, He is steadfast. His provision is everywhere if yet I have eyes to see, ears to hear, a mind to reflect, and a heart to believe. This morning, I felt like I was drowning. But now? I mount up with wings like an eagle and soar (Isa. 40:31). Oh, the very power of the life-breath of the Living God!

11

BREATHE

It's me again, thinking about this whole breathing thing. I read somewhere that the way to expand your lung capacity is by holding your breath. To someone who isn't knowledgeable in all things respiratory, this doesn't quite make sense. You hold your breath to be able to breathe more? I get it, though. I am all too familiar with things not being as they seem, with the very things that appear to be breaking you being the things that are making you stronger. His ways are not our ways, His thoughts not our thoughts (Isa. 55:8). Just because we don't understand something doesn't make it any less true. I don't get how I can pick up a handheld device, push some buttons, and suddenly be talking to (or even looking at) someone halfway across the world. I can't fathom how an act of intimacy intricately forms another human being who, after growing for a few months, is delivered from the body of another and begins their journey on this earth. I don't understand these things, yet I know them to be true from what I've seen. And I think, as Ralph Waldo Emerson once said, that all that I have seen teaches me to trust the Creator for all that I have not seen. He's above it all, you know.

After kicking and flailing around yesterday, I woke up this morning with a soul ready to breathe. If you haven't noticed, I love the mornings. It's quiet, and God's voice is the only thing that seems to be loud in the early dawn hours. There are (usually) no distractions around, and it seems that I can hear His love for me and for you more clearly during these precious moments. I treasure memories of lighting that candle and sitting down on the couch to talk and listen to the God of the universe. It's unbelievable, really, that He gives us the option of doing this—of spending time with the One who made the stars, the sun, and the sky. The consistency of our time together is a comfort like no other; this God, always with us, who meets me wherever I am at because He is, in fact, everywhere I will ever be. The beauty of relationship with Him is that while I am ever changing, He is not. He's always the same, perfect Rock of a God. It's beautiful when you let your mind breathe enough to think about it.

We use bottles to flush the girls' medications or add extra amounts of fluid to their diet. This morning, as I filled the bottle up, I noticed that it read something on its side: First Essentials. I laughed, thinking about how many years we have used the very thing that was made to be seasonal. Why do we do this in Western culture? Why do we call something like an instrument that holds required nutrients a first essential? Why do we constantly feel the need to add more things to the necessary list that aren't really necessary at all? I'm convinced that going on an overseas mission trip changes you. The service and people itself are a huge component of this; however, even just getting out of our day-to-day grind and being busy in a different capacity plays a role. Three and a half weeks in Bangladesh impacted my life more than hundreds ever have. I know God is no less present and real in the here and now; I just think experiencing Him outside of the tangibles we normally walk in helps us to see Him more.

I remember sitting in one of the villages, drinking my instant coffee that had been warmed up by the water that one particular woman (who I have mentioned in many of my writings before) had drawn up from a river at least a mile away. I watched another lady hanging clothes to dry. I saw a child chasing a rooster. There were several men carrying several baskets of produce down to the city. In ways, I felt like I was in a movie. This place—that had no technology, no running water, no need for transportation—was so foreign to me, yet, in the same sense, I felt like it was somewhere I had been before. It seemed like I saw God everywhere—in the woman who tirelessly brought up water for us to purify, getting up at 3:00 AM to bring up gallon after gallon. God was in the lady hanging her family's clothes— probably one of two outfits that they owned, hence the seemingly constant washing—on the clothesline to dry. In all these mundane things, it seemed as if God was somehow nearer than He was in the hustle and bustle of American life. I knew that wasn't true, yet it began to become so obvious why it appeared that way. In America, we think of these everyday tasks as nuisances in the way of getting the real work done. We use machines that accomplish basic needs faster than our two own hands in the hopes of being able to get on to the next thing at a quicker rate. We have devices that supposedly connect us more relationally, yet many of us could not tell you the names of our very neighbors. We are obsessed with being knowledgeable about all the things, yet some of us could not tell you what's going on in the hearts of our closest friends. We are, point-blank, lost in all the distraction and busyness that we claim is living. At times, I think we are missing the point altogether. There is so much beauty in putting down our hurry and relaxing in the daily tasks. There is joy to be found in merely focusing on what America would call the first essentials. These things don't have to be obstacles to true life. In fact, maybe if we focused more on letting God be God—letting Him add whatever He chooses to our plates but obediently living in the places that God has placed us in—maybe we would find our souls breathing more deeply and soundly, after all. A fuller plate does not mean a fuller life—oh, that we would have eyes and hearts to see this!

As I finished filling up the baby bottle, I smiled. My soul felt content and open as I moved on to put medications in the many syringes that had been laid out the night before. I hung the feeding bags on the feeding poles, taking a little extra time to just think about the beauty of doing anything at all. I breathed in one deep breath and exhaled just as slow, going up the stairs to get Ally and Bailey Grace out of their beds to begin the day.

12

STRENGTH IN THE BATTLE

Last night, I looked up various mental-health diagnoses on the Internet. I remember spending a lot of time doing this during graduate school. After learning about all the different codes the DSM had to offer, it seemed like maybe I could fit into several categories. Sure, there were a handful that I couldn't check one or two boxes on, but the rest had me feeling like maybe I was one hard circumstance away from a breakdown. I blush as I admit this—yet we do this with our health often, don't we? We have a weird symptom here and there, nothing too abnormal, but if we take the time to look it up on Dr. Google, we are suddenly convinced we have more going on with us than we ever realized.

If you look at our girls' medical records, they have a list as long as the pages that I type on of different diagnoses. I always put it all under the obscure title of "HECW2," but, really, I could not count on both hands the things that we have been told they have. It's an issue of identity, really. All the things listed are really just symptoms. They don't define Ally or Bailey Grace. I feel this way about a lot of labels we give. The truth is, while I wholeheartedly believe defining an ongoing problem is a great way to treat it, I also think there are a lot of us out here who would do well to simply take emotions and circumstances and good or bad days as they come. We live in a world that spends a lot of time forming identities out of things that were never meant to define us. My human nature struggles with feeling anxious. I don't always feel this way, but there are times and situations that cause me to physically tense up and long to reach for control. For years, I simply said, "It's just the way I am." During those same years, spending time in God's Word and marinating in truth caused me to realize that just because I have the tendency toward something doesn't mean I have to live that way. Because of Christ, we are able to step out of our "I was born this way" into "See, I am doing a new thing" (Isa. 43:19). Because of Christ, we can find strength in the battle, but we have to take the time to recognize what (or Who) we need to clothe ourselves in so that we can do so. Let me explain.

I have spent many seasons recognizing the problem (anxiety), and instead of laying it down at God's feet and letting Him change me, I have covered it up with the temporal Band-Aids of this world. It's tricky, really, because if we clothe ourselves with fleeting pleasures or comforts long enough, we might actually think we have dealt with the issue itself. Anyone following me? I have talked about go-to's before, the things that we use to bring happiness or squelch pain outside of God Himself. Some of us have more than others—often using something that isn't bad in itself but is detrimental when falsely used—but we all have false gods and idols that we are tempted to run to from time to time. What are yours? I want you to take a minute—maybe even put down this book and step to a quiet(er) place—and ask God to reveal your go-to's. There are the obvious ones—drugs, alcohol, sex, food, materialism. But what about the hidden idols of the heart? Do you find yourself listening to praise music most of the time, yet when something hard happens, the station changes? Do you keep certain treats hidden away from the rest of the family, only to be pulled out on a hard day? When someone hurts your feelings, do you stuff the hurt away and lash out instead? Do you have a certain person from the past that you find yourself looking up on social media whenever the day has been hard? When you begin to feel overwhelmed, do you curl up on the couch in front of Netflix and isolate instead of reaching out? Remember, the only way we are able to clothe ourselves with something (Someone) different is when we bring our false robes to the Light. And the only way we can bring these into the Light is by reflecting on what they are in the first place. Don't forget: we do this to experience more freedom, not enslavement. The fact is, it was for freedom that we were set free (Gal. 5:1). In Christ, we are free to battle brokenness and pain and suffering with weapons that last. Remember when Adam and Eve were in the Garden, before the fall happened? Genesis 2:25 says that they were naked and felt no shame. They were stripped of all the things that would hinder them from experiencing true satisfaction in their Creator; and in their authenticity, they did not feel trapped. This is what Christ has accomplished for each of us! In Him, we are able to be figuratively naked, scraped of all the things that would offer short-term "help" for all the hurts and emptiness we feel (including our own sin) in order to be reconciled to the One who offers eternal hope—the perfect Healing Balm—for our weary souls. This, my friends, is how we battle. Our fight is not against flesh and blood (Eph. 6:12), so it makes sense that we can't battle with that. We need Jesus. We need to strip ourselves of all that hinders (Heb. 12:1) and clothe ourselves with Christ Himself. It is then, and only then, that we will be able to see clearly the battle in front of us. We don't lay aside the weights that hinder, only to find ourselves naked and vulnerable. We put these things off in order to put on the things of eternity—the things that last. So when I feel anxious, instead of adding another ridiculous Band-Aid to my already shabby rags, I can lay that anxiety at the feet of Jesus and sense Him clothing me with robes of confidence, robes of righteousness, and robes of peace. If you find yourself feeling hopeless, don't deny it. Don't run to the things of this world that will just add more sadness and pain to your already wounded heart. Run to Jesus! Lay all the hard things at His feet—the things that sting too badly to even speak of—and allow Him to provide hope and healing and joy. He is stronger than all the battles we face, including the greatest ones that often happen inside of our own minds. He has eternally won the war, so I can battle today with the strength of the One who already has the victory.

When Bailey Grace wakes up on a Monday morning, already in the midst of a seizure, He battles for me. When Hugh doesn't respond to my hurting heart like I wished he would, and I'm tempted to not press in, He battles for me. No matter the circumstance, we must battle with all that we are—heart, mind, and strength—knowing that we do not do it on our own! It is Christ in us—the Spirit of the Living God—working out all things for His glory and our good. If we are going to love Him with all our heart, mind, soul, and strength, we are going to need His help with every breath and at every twist and turn. As Elisabeth Elliot once said, "The secret is Christ in me, not me in a different set of circumstances." Today I pray that we do not look to the Internet or another diagnosis to define what's going on in our hearts. My prayer is that we aren't tempted to cover up our mess and that, instead, we would cling to the One who is steadfastly and eternally holding on to us. Our identity is in Him. May we rest in this today and always. Battle on, dear one.

Author's note: I do not want any of this to discount what a mental-health professional has told you. I do pray that you will examine your heart and mind and ask God to make it clear how He would have you handle the wrestlings and thorns of your flesh. He is faithful.

13

SHE IS ME

We get into the car. It is a Wednesday, the day of the week in which the girls currently do not go to school, and I am left with "What are we going to do to entertain everyone today?" Many times, just like so many areas of our life, we do similar things—things that may appear mundane but that bring the girls joy. So often in this home, we delight in feedback. We love to see the girls responding to whatever is in front of them that communicates they are fully present and aware of their surroundings. On this day, I decided to take the girls to the fountain. While November, it's a southern November, the kind where the leaves peak in orange, red, and yellow, and the air feels comfortable enough to be outside without a jacket. It is the perfect weather for the girls, weather that doesn't make their brain respond in shutdown. So to the fountain (albeit the outlet mall) we go.

I roll down the windows, letting the wind blow in our hair, and I turn up the music fairly loud. It's the praise and worship station, Bailey Grace's favorite. It takes her a minute, but slowly she begins to "sing." I use quotations because, while she's not saying the words, while the tune is completely off, it is very clear that she is in fact singing. She starts when the song begins and stops when it stops. It's gloriously appropriate, and I truly feel like she is an angel on earth while she's doing it. Last Christmas Eve, at my parents' mostly conservative church, she began singing (loudly) right as they turned off the lights to sing Silent Night and pass around the candles. It's funny because, really, I think God was probably most pleased at her worship than anything, but as the stares began to come to the back row, we realized we probably needed to take her out so as not to disturb anyone from enjoying their traditional Christmas Eve moment. Because I am convinced mom guilt is a real thing, I whispered to her over and over that her singing was beautiful and that I was so proud to be her mom.

One of the first things that made us realize our girls were different was the fact that their little hands tremored anytime we tried to help them hold on to a toy. Just like everything else, we tried not to look into too much and just named it unusual. Fast-forward a few months and a few "there is something really wrong" doctors' appointments, and the tremoring hands turned into just not grabbing anything at all. I spent months, alongside our therapists, trying to manipulate the girls' hands in order to have them hold on to an object in front of them. I remember the first time I realized that one of the girls was in fact grabbing something. We were at our pediatrician's office, and as he was examining Ally, she reached up and grabbed his stethoscope. My eyes got as big as saucers, and I checked the inch stone box of "grabs object in front of her" in my mind. As months went on, grabbing stuff turned into grabbing stuff and throwing it. These days, we have been working on teaching Bailey Grace and Ally to not only reach for something but also to intentionally keep it in their grasp. We have been doing this for probably almost two years now. The other day, I read Ally's daily school report. Under this particular goal, it said, "Held on to maraca 15 seconds." Fifteen seconds! I couldn't believe it. I texted Ms. Alisha to confirm that one had not accidentally made its way in front of the five and that this in fact had happened. I was floored and texted Hugh a picture of it.

I could list out a handful of other things unique to our girls that make Hugh and me smile with pride—things that the rest of the world would see as simple but we see as monumental. Why? *Because we know them.* We know them, and we love them, and we recognize how challenging this seemingly tiny tasks really are for them. When Bailey Grace sings, I would not dream of thinking she should change her tune or formulate more than a babble. The thought of comparing her to a world-famous singer is preposterous. When Ally holds on to a maraca for 15 seconds, I'm not wondering why she will not build a tower of Legos or stack a set of rings. I am just celebrating her as is, being the best version of who she was created to be. As I was marinating on these things yesterday, I had a stark realization that truly, this is each of us. I am she, she is me. I am a little child, fumbling around this earth, attempting to allow God's Spirit to live through me. I am constantly making mistakes and reading something one minute and then forgetting it the next, and God looks at me with love and says, "This is my child, with whom I am well pleased." Why? Not because I have it all together (quite the opposite). Not because I am checking all the right boxes, or because compared to my neighbor, I am fairing out okay. He looks at me this way because of His Son. He sees me like this because I am His child, and He loves me. The Gospel reminds me that my works and performance are rags compared to a holy God. It shows me that He is fully aware that my actions, thoughts, and abilities are not going to cut it, so thanks be to God, He made a way for me. He made a way for me to be in relationship with Him, and when He sees me, He doesn't expect for me to be anything but me. You and I are made in His image. He loves us! He truly loves us! We can sing off-key; we can drop the maraca before the second mark hits two, and His love for us doesn't change. He isn't interested in us being like the man or woman next door. He wants me—He wants you—as we are. Yes, He will do some molding. At times, He is going to break in order to bind, wound in order to heal; yet, don't mistaken His making you who He already sees you as for lack of love! He loves me, He loves you, the same today as yesterday. The same yesterday as tomorrow. Not because of who we are but because of who He is. She is me and He? He loves us both fiercely and unconditionally not because of who we are but because of who He is.

What a mysteriously steadfast God we serve!

14

HE DOES NOT FAIL

Hugh and I spent the weekend in New York City, just the two of us. We laughed, we cried, we walked, we ate, and we did all the things a tourist is supposed to do in less than 48 hours. The week before, I had practically held my breath in anticipation of whether or not the girls would be well and we would be able to go. It has been months since they have had a respiratory illness, and with every day that passes that they don't have one, it seems more likely that the next day they will.

I have never really enjoyed flying. I do not think about it for days prior to an actual trip, but once I get on the plane, my blood pressure rises, and I begin counting down the minutes until the plane lands again. This unsaid fear bothers me. I read where it says in Proverbs 31:25 that a godly woman "laughs at the time to come," and I cannot help but realize my own deficit in this. If I look back on my week, it seems like many of my moments were spent taking the future way too seriously. I tell myself that if I just knew what was around the corner, regardless of what it was, I wouldn't be so anxious about it, yet I'm not sure this is really true. Isn't the nature of trusting God, believing that the mere fact that He will be around the corner should be enough for us to rest easy? Do I really believe this, or am I giving lip service? Some of the most important questions we could ever ask ourselves are the ones we tend to skirt around in our minds.

This morning, with the girls back in school and my feet planted firmly in our home, I opened up to Hebrews 3:12 and read it:

"Take care brothers, lest there be in any of you an
evil, unbelieving heart, leading you to fall away from
the living God."

I tend to think of evil as ISIS. As murder and slander and greed and complacency. Yet His Word is making it clear that lack of trust and confidence in the Sovereign God is where true evil stems from. If I want to pursue good and neglect the bad, I would be wise to pay more attention to my heart.

So back to the plane. I was annoyed at myself for not being able to relax and decided—even said it aloud to Hugh—that I was determined to feel calm during our flight. We always say truth trumps feelings; but if we are honest, if we have full confidence in what we say is truth, won't our emotions follow? So here I was, doing the only thing I knew to do: Bible open, turning to verse after verse about His care over us. The problem is, every time I got to verses that spoke of Him keeping me from all harm, I remembered all too clearly that the only guarantee in that was Him keeping my soul from harm. Was that enough for me to be at peace? If not, as a professing follower of Christ, shouldn't it be? Maybe the underlying issue wasn't that I didn't trust He was in control. Maybe the deeper problem was that I cared way too much about my earthly life than I wanted to admit.

I kept the verses coming, turning to chapter after chapter about God's goodness toward us. We hit a few bumps, and I gripped the seat tightly. I sighed. "Oh ye of little faith…" I mumbled to myself. The pilot came on the intercom and let us know we were descending as he instructed the flight attendants to prepare for landing. I looked over, saw the ground below, and felt immediate relief. I scolded myself for not experiencing this throughout my time in the air and hung my head in shame, realizing that I was about to put my Bible up and begin to focus on shops, sights, and earthly treasures. And then it hit me. In the same chapter of Hebrews, I read this:

"Therefore...consider Jesus...who was faithful to Him who appointed Him."

(Heb. 3 pieces of verses 1 and 2)

Consider Jesus.

It was all I needed to read to remember why I believed what I believe in the first place. The reality was that yes, my faith was small, yet my God has always been and will always be big. True, I couldn't get it together enough to trust Him on a simple two-hour plane flight, yet He accomplished all that I needed to have life and life eternal. Consider Jesus, the One who has not and cannot and will not ever fail. Yes, I was going to falter, yet His strength was greater than any weakness of my own. I smiled, realizing my blood pressure was down and we were, in fact, technically still in the air. There would be something right around the corner that caused it to go right back up—and there will be for you too. But that's okay because "thanks be to God for His indescribable gift" (2 Cor. 9:15). Consider Jesus, dear heart, and consider Him again and again and again. To Him be the glory.

15

NEVER GRAY

If you have not noticed, the girls and I go on a lot of walks. Our neighborhood is perfect for it—lots of sidewalks and circles, passing playgrounds, and people. And hills. Many, many, hills. I don't like to think about it, but I know our time to be able to do this just the three of us is fleeting. The combination of me getting older and them getting bigger is one that isn't a stranger to my thoughts, and I genuinely cherish the times I get to push them on my own as we sing and pray and simply enjoy creation together. His provision is sure.

Yesterday, as I was pushing Ally and Bailey Grace around, I couldn't help but notice the conglomeration of decorations. It is late November, the time of year where (in the South) the weather seems "just right"—not too hot and not too cold. Some people are holding on to pumpkins and turkey, others are pressing fast-forward into reindeer and twinkling lights. The reality is, while many feel very passionate about said rules on this, there isn't a right or wrong. (Unless we are talking about a real versus a fake Christmas tree, we all know real is the only way, guys). Being serious here, while we make social constructs for these things, we can technically do whatever we want to when it comes to what we choose to decorate our homes with, and no one can tell us otherwise! We have a wooden pallet Christmas tree that is made by a dear friend of my mother-in-law, and last year we kept it up until February. We just couldn't quite put it in the attic, and, let's be honest, we can celebrate Jesus's birth year round, right?

While looking at both the harvest scenes and the winter wonderlands, I started thinking about my own heart and the various seasons of life. There are certain things that are unique to moms with special needs, but there are also universal truths about young motherhood. In this particular season, many of us are somewhat isolated to our homes and simply doing our best to keep husbands and children and homes basically sane. If you are a mom with children under five, I can guarantee that there are days that the only adult conversation you have concerns meal planning and sleep training. It's just the season of life we are in. I think back on college. During that time, most of my days were spent socializing or studying. I could go months without seeing a child. I had more than enough time to work out, and when I was thinking about dinner, the only person I was concerned with pleasing was the one in the mirror. In ways, it was a glorious time. In other ways, it was an unrealistic representation of "real life" moving forward. Regardless, it served its purpose. I can remember going to a park near the main campus and spending hours in God's Word, reading Scripture and journaling and writing down encouraging quotes. Some of those morning (okay, in mom world, really midday) appointments with God still affect my understanding of His promises and His grace. Point-blank, however short of a season it was, it mattered. In God's kingdom, all seasons matter and serve great purpose.

We spend a lot of our lives somewhere in the in-between. We balance pumpkins and snowmen and throw a cupid in the mix. We are happy, and we are sad. We are content, and we are dissatisfied. We are hungry for God and snacking on the world. We boast, and we are humbled. We laugh, and we cry. But God.

> "For everything there is a season, and a time for every matter under heaven: a time to be born, and a time to die; a time to plant, and a time to pluck up what is planted; a time to kill, and a time to heal; a time to

breakdown, and a time to build up; a time to weep, and a time to laugh; a time to mourn, and a time to dance; a time to cast away stones, and a time to gather stones together; a time to embrace, and a time to refrain from embracing; a time to seek, and a time to lose; a time to keep, and a time to cast away; a time to tear, and a time to sew; a time to keep silence, and a time to speak; a time to love, and a time to hate; a time for war, and a time for peace."

(Eccl. 3:1–8)

God promises to bring cause out of everything. He designs each and every millisecond of each and every life according to what brings Him the most glory and His children the most good. Not only that, but also in the midst of our wandering and confusion and smothering of seasons, He is never gray. He is sure. He is steadfast. He absolutely, positively never changes, and He can be trusted. He has a way of pulling together what seems like a broken mess and making a beautiful masterpiece; it's simply who He is. I look around at the yards in our neighborhood, knowing good and well that before I know it, the decorations will be put aside, and the spring flowers will begin to sprout. The beautiful thing? He's making all things new. In the midst of the ever-changing seasons of our lives, one thing can be clung to as the very anchor of our souls: God and His perfect purpose displayed in the love of Jesus Christ and the presence of the Holy Spirit in His people. Cheers to autumn leaves, twinkling wreaths, tulips, summer storms, and everything in the middle, and all glory to the One above it and in it and through it all—to the One who is never gray and always faithful. Amen and amen.

16

THIS IS ME TRYING

I got out of bed as quietly as I knew how, quickly realizing my noise level didn't really matter. We had been up most of the night with Ally smack in between Hugh and me, this time unrelated to coughing. Ally had developed a fever the day before that would not quit despite all of our typical efforts, and her seizures had gotten to the scariest level we had seen under our roof. To go to Children's or not to go to Children's—that was always the question. We had prayerfully decided to wait and keep her close by; both Hugh and I knowing that sleep was not going to be near to either of us. But Ally. Sweet Ally's brain and body had been so taken over by the misfiring of her brain that she almost couldn't stop the sleep from coming. As I got out of bed the next morning, I went into the living room and did the only thing I knew how: talk to God about it all. I prayed, I complained, I asked for forgiveness for my murmuring and disbelief. I reached out to close friends to give an update from what happened throughout the night. These friends—the same ones who had dropped coffee off the night before (knowing good and well that hospital or not, we weren't going to be resting)—were the same ones who had clothes set out ready to go in case they were needed in a pinch. The gift of the Word and the gift of community extends way beyond anything else this earth has to offer.

A few minutes into my time with God, the Holy Spirit was speaking such revelations to my heart. God was breathing peace and comfort and assurance into my very veins, and this unique, often gruesome calling felt like a holy privilege yet again.

Insert approximately thirty minutes later.

Bailey Grace was awake and ready to begin the day. Hugh was up in the study, glued to the Word and unaware of the moaning and groaning from the monitor. The thing about Bailey Grace is that some days she wakes up happy, and some days, for reasons we can't always figure out, she wakes up disgruntled and frustrated. Today, she happened to be in the disgruntled and frustrated mode. After giving her a couple of minutes to make sure she wasn't going to go back to sleep, I went up to her room, stomping up the stairs to make sure Hugh heard me going up, mumbling to myself about how I "just wanted a few more minutes of peace." I brought Bailey Grace down and began our morning routine. Hugh entered the room soon after, on fire to tell me something He had read in God's Word that had encouraged his heart. My flesh reeled and irked for reasons only the spiritual realm could understand. I gave a half-hearted "that's great, babe" back to Hugh while continuing to syringe medications into Bailey Grace's G-tube. Hugh continued with said encouragement. I cut in. "Hey, Hugh, could you go check and make sure Ally is still asleep? We kind of need to be watching her." Hugh looked confused but went in to the room anyway. "Still sleeping. Hey, are you okay?"

Am I okay?

The conversation that followed still causes my cheeks to flush red as I type the words.

"Am I okay? Let's see, Hugh. Our daughter has been seizing basically constantly for over a day. She has had two seizures where she turned blue in the face and—if even for a couple of seconds—we thought she could be dying. We have almost called an ambulance three times since yesterday, and I haven't slept enough for it to count. So, no. No, I'm not okay."

This woman. This same woman who less than an hour prior had been "filled with the Holy Spirit" and "at peace with whatever lot the Lord saw fit" as seen in her journal. This woman would be me, and those words were directed toward my husband. My godly, loving, gentle husband who had been experiencing the same reality I had for the past 24 hours. Hugh, relying on the Spirit I'm sure, didn't seem to take it personally and didn't say a word back. I began to take dishes out of the dishwasher, embarrassed not just about what I had said but mainly what it revealed about my heart. I left the room and began folding laundry (another escape method of mine) and repented to the Lord for the dark places of my heart that I had been refusing to let the light enter in to. I walked back into the room.

"Hey, Hugh?"

"Yes, babe?" His tone was so kind, so undeserved.

"I'm really sorry not just for what I said but for the way I said it. The fact is, as sad as this might sound, this is me trying." As I said the words, I realized just how true they were. My flesh was physically and emotionally drained, and, truly, I wasn't trying to make our house any more volatile than it already felt.

"I know," Hugh responded short and sweet but in a way that made me believe he really did validate I was trying. "This is hard, Morgan. It's just all really hard. I know you are trying, and you're doing a great job of it."

You might read the above and find it easy to give me grace. You might be thinking, *Morgan, under the circumstances and the trauma and lack of sleep and all the things, it makes total sense you would be irritable.* But what about the person who cuts you off in traffic? What about that coworker who seems to change the vibe of the office just by walking in? What about the friend who hasn't responded to your text for the umpteenth time? What about—and, listen closely, because this is an important one—what about the person in the mirror whom you continue to treat differently than you would ever treat someone you love?

I think if we knew each other's stories on any given day, we would be much gentler with one another. The truth is, even on our best days, this world is uncomfortable and hard and simply not our home. And, beyond that, I really do believe that even in the midst of snapshots that look far from it, most of us could look at those in front of us at any given moment and humbly whisper, "Despite what it sounds or looks like, this is me trying."

> Because the reality is that things are only inexcusable
> when we don't understand them.
> In addition, if in Christ—

> "From now on, therefore, we regard no one according
> to the flesh. Even though we once regarded Christ ac-
> cording to the flesh, we regard him thus no longer.
> Therefore, if anyone is in Christ, he is a new creation.
> The old has passed away; behold, the new has come.
> All this is from God, who through Christ reconciled us
> to himself and gave us the ministry of reconciliation."

> (2 Cor. 5:16–18)

I will be the first to admit it: sometimes I confuse the ministry of reconciliation with the ministry of judgment. I forget that I'm not called to be anyone's Holy Spirit; I am called to lead them to Jesus. I was never assigned the job of "Tell everyone you come across where you don't see Jesus in their life," but, instead, I am given the holy privilege of being reconciled to God Himself and overflowing in praise in all that I say, do, and, yes, think.

Friends, let's look back on my mistakes and learn from them instead of repeating them. Yes, let's repent and move forward in grace and truth. Let's ask the Holy Spirit to not just tame our flesh but also crucify it. Yes, let's die to self again and again and again, but when in our weakness and humanity, this just doesn't happen? Grace upon grace upon grace.

> "For God did not send his Son into the world to con-
> demn the world, but in order that the world might be
> saved through him."
>
> > (John 3:17)

We are all going to have bad moments, days, weeks. We are going to go through times that, as Paul says in Romans 7:15, "I do not do what I want, but I do the very thing I hate." But God. As we seek to trust more and more in future grace (John Piper), as we place our trust in Christ and His sufficiency on our behalf instead of our insufficiency within our flesh, He makes us more like Himself not in spite of these moments but including them. He promises us He is using all things for His glory and our good.

> "And we all, with unveiled face, beholding the glory of
> the Lord, are being transformed into the same image
> from one degree of glory to another. For this comes
> from the Lord who is the Spirit."
>
> > (2 Cor. 3:18)

Take heart, beloved. The One who was born fully God, fully man—this Jesus who came down and lived a perfect life and died a horrendous death on the cross —this God who resurrected Himself and dispelled the power of sin and death for all time for everyone who believes, He is seated on the throne and assures us with every ounce of His Holy Being that He is making all things new and that this can be written down, sealed for all time, and trusted for all eternity (Rev. 21:5).

So today? Today when we find the person in front of us (even that stubborn one in the mirror) not looking much like who we think he or she should be; today, when despite all our seemingly best efforts the roast burns (or even more humbling, the frozen pizza); and their words cut deep; the house is a mess; and anything lovely, true, and good seems far, far away, let's remind ourselves that in fact "this is me trying." This is you trying. This is he, this is her trying.

All glory to the One who made it infinitely clear that our efforts will always be rags, and His righteousness is always the answer.

17

MISPLACED SHAME

I opened the cabinet and pulled out a plate; it was solid red. It was next to the smaller plates with Santa Claus on it, with the solid red bowls sitting close by. I pulled out a coffee mug, St. Nick's jolly face staring back at me. It was January 5. I was more than ashamed.

Hugh walked into the kitchen, and as he pulled out a bowl for his cereal, I couldn't help but blurt out, "I'm really sorry, babe. About the bowls, I mean." Hugh stared back, obviously confused. Those of you who are married know that sometimes these situations feel like a tightrope. I could see the wheels of his brain turning:

Am I supposed to know why she's sorry? Is me not knowing a clue I have not listened or heard or something along those lines? He responded with a safe "It's okay, babe" and began to pour his cereal in said bowl.

I knew the cardinal rule: Christmas stuff away at least by January. If not the first, then certainly the second. The truth is, I had thought about putting away the Christmas kitchen décor many times in the past week—I just didn't want to take the time to wrap it all up and lug it up to the attic. We had taken down the tree and placed the manger and snow globe and "JOY" sign in their proper place. What was my problem? I looked to the clutter corner, otherwise known as the Mud Room, and gave another sigh. For probably two months, I had been telling myself I would put not only the beach bag but also the leftover Halloween candy up, but there it all sat. *Why can't I just get it together?* I thought as I got the girls' medications and feeding supplies out. "I'm such a scattered wife and mom. I never follow through with things. Our house is a wreck!" I mumbled to myself as I packed Hugh's lunch and sat Bailey Grace and Ally's school bags out.

Do you ever feel like a failure? I think the answer is probably yes, regardless of how "together" you seem. The truth is, we all have things in our life that we wish were different. There are pieces of my personality, your personality, that seem to not fit in the flow of the rest of our lives. I have a hard time with my tongue. What I mean by this is that I sometimes find it leading me rather than me leading it. I often struggle with the whole James 1:19 command to "be quick to hear, slow to speak, slow to anger." I cannot tell you how many times I've left a conversation and realized I should have cut myself off about two minutes—or sometimes, let's be honest, ten—prior. Anyone relate?

The process of sanctification—this mystery of God making us holy—is just that: a process. The mysterious part is that He tells us to "work out your own salvation with fear and trembling" (Phil. 2:12). This would sound like a complete contradiction to the Gospel we know unless we read the next verse, "For it is God who works in you, both to will and work for his good pleasure" (Phil. 2:13). So we continue to work at holiness knowing that it's the Holy One doing the work?

I believe I should feel grief over my sin. I believe that I should feel ashamed when I fall short of the glory of God. This is not a works-based theology in the least. Let me explain. I am saved—meaning, I am reconciled to God and will spend eternity with Him—by Christ and His death and resurrection alone. It is faith in Jesus and what He accomplished that grants me salvation. Any teaching that suggests otherwise is not the Gospel. Once I begin to grasp this truth and accept it—again, by faith—He begins this work in me called sanctification. I say He begins it, but technically it's already been finished. God is not constrained by time and so He sees all—the beginning, the middle, the end. He sees all and is in all, so trying to find a way to understand or explain what happens in any given state is quite challenging. Because of what Christ did, as the ancient hymn suggests, "No guilt in life, no fear in death, this is the power of Christ in me." So, when I say I believe I should feel grief over my sin, I am not saying I should hold the weight of eternal responsibility for my sin. If that were true, then Christ came for nothing. What I am suggesting, however, is that when I sin, God's Spirit in me (which He promised He gave me the day I began to believe) should announce to my being that whatever I just said, did, thought, was not His best for me. Second Corinthians 7:10 writes this way:

> "For godly grief produces a repentance that leads to salvation without regret, whereas worldly grief produces death."

Godly grief.
A much different kind of sorrow than worldly sorrow.
Worldly sorrow says: You did that thing? You can't be forgiven.
Godly sorrow proclaims: You did that thing? Run back to God, and receive His grace.
Worldly guilt says: You can never overcome this sin.
God says: I overcame it on the cross; now turn from it and turn to me.
The world says: You can never change.
God says: I accomplished all that was needed to make you who I have called you to be.
The world says: Do what you want, and find security in success, beauty, material things, comfort, other people to find true happiness.
God says: True purpose and identity and joy is found in me.

Time and time again, God reminds us in His Word that a grief that pleases Him is a grief that sends us back to His ever-present grace and His never-changing, never-leaving arms.

So what does this have to do with Christmas plates?

I believe that we spend a lot of time feeling bad for things that we were never meant to feel bad for and feeling good about things we were never meant to feel good about. The issue with measuring my success or security on my performance on any given day is that it changes. The problem with determining whether or not I'm doing the right thing based on what the world decides is that there are way too many opinions. The only place we can find complete assurance is at the foot of the cross (which ultimately translates to the throne of God above!). At the cross, we are able to see the love of God displayed for us not because of what we've done but because of who God says we are. At the cross, we are able to watch God Himself overcome the power of death because of what comes next: the Resurrection. At the cross, we are able to recognize without an ounce of fear that because He died and then again was raised on our behalf, our true selves are ultimately hidden with Him (Col. 3:3). This is where our hope lies, not in putting away Christmas decorations or getting a raise or keeping a perfectly tidy house. Our only accolade is Jesus Himself!

I have said it before, and I will say it again: we spend a lot of time talking to God and a lot of time listening to our flesh and the Enemy when we should be doing the opposite. I believe that if we spent more of our energy working toward listening to what God has to say—who we are, who He is, and His promises toward us—we wouldn't have as many holes to fill with the subtle or not-so-subtle lies we let determine our actions and moods. I long to spend more time fixing my eyes on Jesus than I do focusing on the mirror. I desire to be a woman who doesn't have time to think about what plates are in my cabinet simply because I'm opening my heart and home to those around me regardless of bowls or cups or even what's being served as long as I'm offering it with generosity and grace. If I'm exerting my strength to allow Christ to use this jar of clay to serve those around me, I might find my house a bit messier. I might find my sink a little fuller. I could find the Christmas plates up a bit longer. But you know what else will be present?

More of God and less of me.

"...we have this treasure in jars of clay, to show that the surpassing power belongs to God and not to us."

(2 Cor. 4:7)

In light of this, I have a feeling we might be placing fruit salad on St. Nicholas's jolly old face in July.

All for the glory of God, of course.

18

WHAT I WISH FOR YOU

We had some of our dearest friends over for dinner last night. They are the kind of friends who it almost feels insulting to call friends because they are just so much more than that. They are some of the people who show up as equally for the mourning as they do the rejoicing. They have laughed with us and cried with us, oftentimes within the same sentence. I hope you have these friends.

As we sat over hot bowls of soup and crusty bread, we talked about the season of life that each of us are in, and then we both dreamed of the future and processed some of the past. This particular couple are still in the newlywed phase, and as we sat and talked about the whole concept of family, the wife confessed to sometimes fearing not having her version of perfect children. She went on to say that she knew there was no such thing as perfect but that she also was painstakingly aware that she already had a vision of timing and personality and even physical appearance that she was just, point-blank, going to have to die to. Only a dear friend could come in our home and admit these things without it feeling the least bit offense to Hugh and me.

Our dear friends, believe in the same God we do—the One True God. They proclaim Christ as the Way, the Truth, and the Life (John 14:6). Because of this, encouragement comes easy among us. We spent a little time reminding her truths that her head knew but her heart needed repeated: that God would only give her His best. That He would help her die to the things that were not serving Him or her when the time came. Yet, as we were doing this, Hugh chimed in and said, "We know trials are going to come, but, of course, we wouldn't wish this upon anyone."

My heart sank, and my blood pressure rose. "Wait, what?" I spouted back.

Now, it's important to remember that these are the kind of friends who don't get a filter when they come in our house. That being said, I could tell this was going to open a whole new can of worms that maybe none of us had anticipated.

Surely I had misheard Hugh, yet his response led me to realize I was not mistaken in my interpretation.

After a few sentences back and forth, Hugh said, "Morgan, think back on the past few years. You are saying that you would wish all those things on them?"

So, think I did.

It was the very first time either of our girls had been admitted to the hospital. Looking back on it, I'm not sure if I was in denial, naïve, or a healthy combination of both. I have said this before, but I will say it again: I wasn't one of those girls who dreamed about being a mama. In fact, while I babysat a handful of times, I never enjoyed it and, honestly, didn't feel that great at it. (If you are reading, and I babysat your children, your family is an exception to the rule, of course). In all actuality, I have always had a more serious side to me that didn't do so well in situations with silly, carefree young children. I can remember babysitting a little girl once who really didn't want to go to sleep. It was Christmastime, and so, in my youth, it seemed like a totally acceptable thing to tell her that if she didn't go to sleep, Santa Claus wouldn't come. Her response?

"I don't care! I don't want a big ol' stranger coming down my chimney and leaving stuff I don't know about, anyway!"

She had a point.

I found it much easier to sit in my room and write (even as a middle-school girl) than to giggle about the latest silly movie (what was so funny about a dog getting loose and destroying a beautiful, elegant wedding reception as he barged through and—spoiler alert—caused the cake to fall flat to the ground? Nothing. The appropriate answer is nothing. And let's be honest: ruined cake is never something to laugh about). That being said, when I thought about being an adult, my thoughts didn't go much farther than the concept of independence.

I will never forget the first time I changed Ally's diaper. The nurse in the NICU called out, "Hey, mom, you want to change it?" It took me about two minutes to realize that she was talking to me. I was mom. I knew the right thing to say was "of course," but as I slowly walked over to the incubator Ally was in, I realized very quickly that I was not sure I remembered how to change a diaper. My husband and mother-in-law were in there with me, and because they were both pediatricians, in my mind I was the only one who was a rookie in the room. I stumbled around, and approximately three minutes later, this little four-pound baby had a fresh diaper on. I tell you this to say I wasn't exactly the most informed when it came to all things babies.

So, back to the hospital.

Bailey Grace was nine months old, and she had been sick for about 24 hours. At the time, Hugh was a resident, and we were pretty much in the dark about what exactly was going on mutation-wise. We knew that something was "not normal"; we just weren't sure to what extent. So with the girls being sick for the first time (at nine months, God's protection I am sure of it), I didn't really know how sick was too sick. Bailey Grace had been unable to keep any food or drink down, and because this was pre-feeding tubes, we didn't really have any options other than to keep on trying. Back then, I was unaware of respiratory rates or signs of distress or any of the like, but around 4:00 P.M., I called Hugh and told him I thought she might need to be seen. Hugh, thinking I was simply a new mom who had never had a sick child, told me he would meet me at after hours. I got the girls into the car, and as I was pushing their double stroller up to the door, Hugh walked up. The look on his face told me everything.

"Morgan, how long has she looked like this?" he questioned.

It had been a couple of hours, I was sure, and after being triaged and answering a few questions, the physician on staff came in and told us she was going to admit Bailey Grace.

"To the hospital?" I sputtered.

I was confused. I hadn't packed a bag. I thought the hospital was a place for kids who were dying. I know all this may sound crazy, especially with a husband in the medical field, but I truly just had never imagined what the medically fragile life would look like. At the time, I didn't know we were quite literally living it—times two.

Logistics are really important around here, especially during illness. Seventy-five percent of the time, within 12 hours of one girl getting sick, her sister is down as well. We have learned through the years how to navigate it all, but on this first occasion, we were all kind of confused on how to make this happen (we have two cars, we need a bag for the hospital, does Hugh need to call in for work, how sick is Ally, etc.) I remember Hugh looking at me and asking, "Do you want me to stay with her?"

"With Bailey Grace?" I asked back with a tone that suggested he was out of his mind.

Hugh learned very quickly that there was no talking me into leaving "the weakest link" in times like these. Momma bear was not leaving her cub, no matter how exhausted or how many nights in a row that meant. The painful part was—and always is—that Ally needed her momma too. I think God has given me a unique grace to simply not focus on this in the middle of crisis, but I always get teary-eyed as I explain to the one who isn't in the hospital that I love them, that daddy (or whoever is stepping in from the tribe) is going to take good care of them, that I'm praying, and that I promise to do the same for them if needed.

This particular time it was decided that I would drive Bailey Grace to the hospital and that my dear friend Ashley would pack a bag for me at the house and bring it up to the hospital. Bailey Grace was admitted to Special Care, and I will never forget watching three separate nurses try and get an IV started on her very dehydrated fragile body. For a couple of minutes, Bailey Grace cried in a way I had never heard her cry before. Finally, she was too weak and too sick to even cry anymore. She gave me a look that still brings tears to my eyes. It was a look I have seen since then more than a handful of times, a look that said, "Mom, please end this suffering." Any of you who have received this same wordless look from your child know exactly what I mean when I say it was too much. The nurse looked at me and said, "Mom, it's okay if you need a moment. We can take it from here." I felt a lump coming up high in my throat, and the hot tears were about to overflow. I stepped into the bathroom and cried for a few minutes and then dried my tears and came back in. Thankfully, they had finally gotten the IV started, and she was resting. Around an hour later, our first night (of now more than I can count) of coughing and vomiting up blood began.

It was absolutely terrifying, but after the terrible ended, a couple of days later, Bailey Grace was feeling better, and we were finally able to go home. No less than twelve hours after, I went in with Ally. For a few years, this cycle became all too typical in our home.

Do I wish this on my friend?

I will never forget the first night I knew for sure that Bailey Grace was having a seizure. I had been suspicious for a while that they were doing some interesting movements, but an EEG revealed "abnormal" but not concrete information. I had Googled way too many times and videoed way too many moments that my momma gut told me "weren't right." Hugh had always told me that if it was really a seizure, I would just know.

From about the time that the girls were six weeks old up until they were almost three, we hosted a small group in our home for the medical community. Our girls have never been great sleepers and so watching the monitor while attempting to lead or focus on whatever we were discussing in any given moment could present as a challenge.

One night, I looked down at the monitor and noticed Bailey Grace's eyes were open. Her hands were drawn up close to her chest, and something just seemed off. I went upstairs, attempting to not disturb the conversation, and as soon as I got up there, I knew.

"*Hugh!*" I yelled.

Now, at the time, I didn't know that this would be our reality each and every night for years to come. Right then and there, it felt like a true emergency. Hugh came upstairs and, after looking down at Bailey Grace, turned on the light. This first seizure lasted about five minutes (feeling like hours), and when we went downstairs, the small group conversation had dissipated, and a few close friends were standing at the stairway. That same lump and those same hot tears filled up in my eyes. I hugged my friend Sarah and let a few tears roll down before I pulled it together, and Hugh and I talked about a plan of action.

Two nights later, as we went upstairs to be with Bailey Grace while seizing, we looked over at Ally's crib, only to see her doing exactly the same thing. That very week both girls were admitted to the Epilepsy Unit, where we began our journey with medications and pulse ox's and all the like.

Would I wish this upon my friend?

"For it has been granted to you that for the sake of Christ you should not only believe in Him but also suffer for His sake."

(Phil. 1:29)

Granted to you. Given to you as a gift.

"The Spirit Himself bears witness with our spirit that we are children of God, and if children, then heirs—heirs of God and fellow heirs with Christ, provided we suffer with Him in order that we may also be glorified with Him. For I consider that the sufferings of this present time are not worth comparing with the glory that is to be revealed in us."

(Rom. 8:16–18)

Provided that we suffer with Him in order to be glorified with Him. Sufferings that don't compare with the glory that will be revealed.

"Therefore let those who suffer according to God's will entrust their souls to a faithful Creator while doing good."

(1 Pet. 4:19)

Suffer according to God's will.

Just like I didn't think much about being a mom prior to becoming pregnant, I didn't meditate much on suffering prior to finding out our daughters had severe special needs. The truth is, while I had walked through "some stuff," I had not done so well. What I mean by that is that I hadn't "entrusted my soul to a faithful Creator while doing good" in the midst of the suffering. I had fought it. I had escaped it. But I had never simply rested in the goodness of God in the midst of hard things. When we first realized that Ally and Bailey Grace were going to be differently abled, I knew I had to make a choice. Sunday-school answers were not going to cut it anymore. I was going to have to choose to trust God, to keep my hands and heart open to whatever He chose for the girls and for Hugh and me, or I was going to fall into the trap of disowning truth and forgetting the sovereignty of the Living God in the middle of it all. The grace of God enabled me to choose the first, and it has changed my days forever. My flesh is still there, and as Psalm 73 so poignantly points out, it still fails. Yet God. He takes my mustard-seed faith and gives me a Philippians 4 peace that passes understanding in return. At the end of the day, I no longer fear the big things, and it's not because I have some big faith on my own.

> "For the righteous will never be moved; he will be re-membered forever. He is not afraid of bad news; his heart is firm, trusting in the Lord. His heart is steady; he will not be afraid, until he looks in triumph on his adversaries."

> (Ps. 112:6–8)

Because of Christ, because of what He did on the cross, because of the greater reality that He was raised from the dead, because He has enabled me in faith to accept and believe this, I am declared righteous. If those statements are true about you as well, then you too are called righteous in Jesus's name. Because of all this, I will be remembered forever. To word it another way, God's attention will forever be on me. Nothing can happen outside of His good, loving hand and plan. Knowing this, bad news isn't eternally bad. With awareness of this, I can move forward with a steadfast heart in all things, knowing that if He has allowed it, He is going to use it. Nothing is wasted in the Kingdom of God, and one day we will look in triumph on the

Enemy of our souls, knowing that Jesus paid it all. I would not know this with every ounce of my being without the journey that we have walked through with our girls. Each piece of the puzzle, especially the hard ones, have brought me to greater belief in these precious truths. In the beginning of it all, I wondered why. I didn't understand why some people had certain trials and others seemed to get through this life with only a couple of bumps in the road. Now, by the grace of God, I see it for what it truly is: a holy privilege. You see, I now believe suffering isn't a punishment but an invitation to know God more deeply and participate in the glorious process of making Him known. The God I know fiercely sticks with me, and with you, in the middle of anything and everything He ordains. He is Immanuel, God with us.

So, do I wish a greater and deeper knowledge of this
on my friend?
Absolutely.

In the past five years, Hugh and I have walked through some of the hardest moments of our lives. I have felt nauseous—literally nauseous—over the amount of moments I have spent watching my daughters suffer.

But God?

He has watched His children suffer more. Beyond that, He sent and watched His Son suffer more than I could ever possibly imagine or bear. And if He used that to bring the greatest glory there ever was or ever has been up until this time, surely He can bring glory and good out of these moments too.

In light of this, the truth is that I wish not a second more or a second less of tribulation on my friend than our perfectly loving, perfectly present Father ordains. God is God, and I am not, and that is a good, good thing.

O Lord, may thy will be done.
At all times. In all things. No matter what.
In my life and in yours, forever.
Amen.

19

FIRST WORLD PROBLEMS

This will hopefully be the most first world problem chapter you will ever read. Or that I will ever write. Or maybe both. Let me start by saying most of what I'm going to write about has to do with going to World Market as a family and buying a futon (and some cute bohemian pillows). Yeah. Let's start there.

It's the middle of one of the coldest winters I can remember. It's also the middle of one of the most potent flu seasons I can recall. Last Saturday, we had been cooped up in the house for one too many hours (only a true Southern writer would include the word "cooped" in her writing repertoire. Bless my heart). Hugh and I both decided that it was time to fulfill our "movie room" dreams. I have this in quotation marks because I love to use them and look for opportunities to do so; I also used quotation marks because the section of our home I'm talking about isn't exactly a room and is more appropriately called a hallway. It's big enough for a television, toys, and sitting options, however; and so Hugh and I had been dreaming about making it an area for movie watching for the girls (and for us. Totally for us too, but it always makes you feel better to put bigger expenses as a gift to your kids, right?). So here we were on a typical January weekend, trying to find things to do. We got into the car and looked around at a couple of places, not finding anything that truly fit the space (clearly, this was a hard day for us). As we were driving past World Market, I saw the sign—a message from God Himself, of course—"Up to 60% ALL furniture!"

Hugh screeched into the handicap spot as if it was Black Friday, and there was no time to waste, and in we went. We walked to the back, and as we did, we saw it.

The perfect futon.

It was perfect for multiple reasons. Perfect because it was not too big and not too small but mainly perfect because it was 50 percent off, and we were in need of a project. After watching another family walk over to it, take a couple of glances at the price, and have their six-year-old little boy sit and lay on it to "try it out," Hugh and I looked at each other and nodded and then I walked over to the closest cashier. I knew what I needed to do. I let him know we were ready to purchase our "perfect futon." (I also committed to Lysoling the thing in its entirety before it set foot in our house. Who knows how many germ-infested six-year-olds had sat down on that thing). We decided to get the pillows that were displayed because, well, why not? We picked out a rug because, suddenly, this frugal couple was having a moment, and this space had to be finished (for Ally and Bailey Grace's sake, of course). We took the tag to the front, awkwardly trying to hold pillows and rugs and push wheelchairs all at the same time. After scanning it all, the cashier looked at us and told us we could pull our car to the front and they would wheel it out and help us get it in our vehicle.

To our van, to be exact.

This van that was going to hold multiple pillows and a rug and two wheelchairs and, oh, two adults and two children as well.

"Sounds good," Hugh responded casually.

Now, anyone who has been married for more than a few minutes knows that to tell your husband he is wrong about, well, anything is not the best idea. I was quite sure that while our perfect futon was not too big and not too small for the movie hallway, it was not going to be able to be stuffed into our already full minivan.

So I said nothing.

We got to the van and put all said items in, and Hugh drove up to the front of the store. Cashier guy came out wheeling the perfect futon, took one look at the van, and said, "How's this going to work?"

Hugh gave a special analysis of how the whole thing was going to go down, and cashier guy, like any smart cashier guy would do, simply nodded and lifted where he was told. After attempting to fit it in "like so," a third of the perfect futon was still hanging out.

"Awesome. Thanks for your help!" Hugh said.

Cashier guy, looking as confused as I was feeling, said what any good cashier guy should:

"You're welcome!"

And just like that, he walked away.

Hugh looked at me, I looked at Hugh, and he simply said, "All right, babe, you can get into the car."

With the back of the van wide open.

With the perfect futon hanging out the back.

Good wife went out the door.

"I'm sorry, what? You can't possibly think we are going to drive home with that thing hanging out. It's going to fall—"

Before I could finish my sentence, Hugh cut in defensively, sounding half offended and somewhat laughing, "No, it won't. I am going to sit in the back, you are going to drive. Just trust me."

Ouch.

Anytime you hear "Just trust me" as a wife, you know the results could go either way, but your response has to be the same.

"Okay."

I got in the driver's seat, Hugh climbed between the girls and grabbed onto the perfect futon, and off we drove. The looks from cars around us ranged from "Let me speed up to get away from whatever's going on here" to "Let me slow down to give these people a look that says, 'You realize you are driving on a main road with a futon hanging out the back of your minivan, right?' My favorite people, though, were the ones who gave me a glance that said, "Girl,

I get it. You have some extra baggage, and you need some room." No questions asked, they just gave me a side smile and then gave me some space.

We didn't get the girls wheelchairs until they were three years old. Prior to that, we would go into the grocery store and receive absolutely no special attention. If I left the double stroller in the middle of the aisle for a second too long, someone would ask me to move it (sometimes kindly, sometimes not). If I had too much stuff piled into the bottom of the stroller, often the person at the register would give me funny looks. If one of the girls was making atypical noises as we walked through the store, all the perturbed looks would ensue.

The first day I took the girls out by myself in their wheelchairs, I went to Target (because no chapter titled "First World Problems" would be complete without a mention of Target). I can't tell you how different the response has been from that trip forward. I genuinely think I could steal someone's grocery cart piled high with all their favorite things and they would just let me do it. One time, I accidently took way too long choosing coffee creamer (it's a hard choice, okay?) and blocked the aisle for a good five minutes. (Two wheelchairs side by side take up a ton of space). After choosing, I glanced up and saw that three people were just waiting for me to move but hadn't said a word. Who knows how long they had been waiting. "Oh goodness, I'm so sorry!" I apologized.

"You have *nothing* to be sorry about!" one of the three responded.

"Yeah, seriously! You did nothing wrong!" said another.

"You're an incredible mom!" the third joined in.

Hypothetically speaking, there was a futon hanging out the back of my van, and it was obvious I needed some grace.

Am I making sense to anyone?

"Out of my distress I called on the Lord, the Lord answered me and set me free."

(Ps. 118:5)

As laughable as it is, having the perfect futon hanging out the back of the minivan felt stressful to me. What if it actually fell out? What if it caused a wreck? What if we got pulled over? On a smaller scale, what if people kept staring at us as if we had lost our minds?

Because I was at least aware that being distressed about a silly couch was slightly ridiculous, I started to think about this concept of distress. The truth is, sometimes my distress is caused by relatively unimportant things, but sometimes my distress looks like standing in the middle of Ally and Bailey Grace's bedroom, watching both of them seize as I try to figure out who needs me the most in that moment (Who is the most clammy? Who is tremoring more? Who looks fearful like maybe they are in desperate needs of simply holding their momma's hand?). It's comforting to know that God is with me in both of those moments. That when He says we can "cast all our anxiety on Him," it's not because our anxiety is warranted; it's "because He cares for you" (1 Pet. 5:7). Maybe He tells us He will be with us in our distresses, not necessarily because the actual thing is stressful but because our emotions in any given moment can be just plain off, and He wants us to know He is with us, even in those seemingly off moments.

We got home with the perfect futon. I used maybe half a can of Lysol to spray it down and let it air out before we brought it in to the movie hallway. Later that night, we turned on a Disney movie and watched it all together as the girls kicked and giggled on the new rug, and Hugh and I sat on our glorified couch (they pull out, you know). Looking back on the drive home, the whole thing felt silly. But isn't that how most things in life feel, and if they don't feel that way now, don't we realize they probably will later?

> "Strength and dignity are her clothing, and she laughs
> at the time to come."

> (Prov. 31:25)

I so want to be this woman—this Proverbs 31 woman who doesn't fear the future and doesn't make light things too heavy and simply wakes up carefree with hands and heart open to whatever God has planned; but so often I find myself in distress over things that simply don't matter. Yet He is with me in my distresses. He is with you in your distresses. And, whether little or big, He asks us to cast our cares on Him because He truly cares. Maybe each and every circumstance we have walked through or are going to walk through is just one more opportunity to take His ever-present hand and confidently say, "Lord, I trust You." Because God knows all things and is bringing good out of everything He allows—maybe the only proper response in the midst of our distress is to recognize our inaccurate, faulty perception of whatever is in front of us and let Him do the work. And you know what? The good news is this: I think Jesus coming down is the truest, trustiest sign that He's committed to being with us no matter what—perfect futon hanging out the back and all.

20

GOD WITH US

I saw it in my rearview mirror.

Every day, the girls are wheeled to our van, while the other kids wait to be walked to their car. I park in a handicap spot to the side of the school, and I get to watch their last interactions with peers and teachers. On this particular day, a birthday was being celebrated. As the girls were being pushed away, the mother of the child whose birthday it was got all the students together for a group picture. Ally and Bailey Grace were not in it, and it was obvious no one noticed. A place in my heart that goes much farther than explanation ached deeply as I watched them all crowd together and smile. Bailey Grace and Ally—whether they were aware or not—kicked and smiled as they simply enjoyed the moment. I took a slow breath in and out and got out of the car to greet the girls and hear about their day.

We live in an incredibly neat neighborhood, the kind that mimics how things used to be. We know most of our neighbors, and it's not uncommon to see children riding their bikes with a friend on the sidewalks or families walking dogs and pushing wagons toward the playground. There is even an ice-cream truck that comes around in warmer months—creepy carnival music and all. We have gotten to know several families in our circle, and we often meet up in the park when weather tolerates to mingle and—for most—allow the kids to play with one another. When the girls were younger, there were a few babies in the crowd, and blankets would be laid out in the grass so that they could kick around and entertain themselves. These days, most of the kids are at an age where running around and playing with the latest outdoor toys is preferred. Several families have blow-up bouncy houses that are set up from time to time. It's beautiful, really.

But for me?
For me, if I'm just plain honest, it's hard.
Really, really hard.

The thing about Bailey Grace and Ally is that they want to be included. You can see it in their eyes as kids run by—they dart their heads and kick their legs and move their arms as if to say, "Me! I want to play too! Come play with me!" The kids, for the most part, are perfectly cordial with the girls, but do they have a friendship? I can't really answer yes to that. A lot of times, a child will walk to Ally and Bailey Grace and say hello in a formal "my mom asked me to do this" kind of tone. They will check that box off before running away on to the next thing. The grace my girls offer is so unconditional, so generous, so Christlike. They always give a wave, smile, or excited look back as if to say, "You noticed me! Thank you so much." I too try to praise any acknowledgment another child gives my girls—mainly because I want it to happen as many times as possible. I find myself feeling like a momma bird watching her nest in these situations. I don't leave Bailey Grace and Ally's side. I stand by their wheelchairs and include them in on any conversation I'm having—usually words and topics way beyond their years. It is one of the reasons I feel like they are old souls despite developmentally being labeled intellectually disabled or whatever the politically correct phrase for cognitively delayed has been named currently. After a while, they, understandably, get bored of adults and tired of sitting up. I too get worn—emotionally exhausted—by the whole setting. Usually, this is when we decide it's time for us to leave. I make sure to walk over to the kids, particularly the ones who initially said hello, so that the girls can say bye. I'm not sure why, but it always feels like the right thing to do. The nice kids will stop what they are doing for a couple of seconds and say good-bye to Ally and Bailey Grace, their parents giving them a nod of approval for their act of kindness. I am actually beginning to cry as I type this because I have never articulated it all in this way, yet it is so very true.

I want to make it clear that I don't think there is anyone to blame in either of these situations. Truly, nothing is being done wrong per se; it's simply the way that things are. Those of you who have kids with special needs most likely know exactly what I'm talking about because we are faced with situations like this every single day, and I'm sure the older the girls get, the more circumstances we will have. Kids will start having sleepovers and playdates—not exactly a place where feeding tubes and unexplained vomiting and seizures belong. Ally and Bailey Grace have so much to offer; they are so full of joy and such heartfelt companions. A part of me feels like if anyone deserves friendship, it would be them. I feel silly even admitting this, but I have sometimes wondered that if ever there is a child who looks past the medically fragile surface and sees within and wanted to invite them over to play if I could ask a nurse to come along so that they would be able to go without me. Bigger, hot, wet tears flow down my cheeks now as I recognize the reality that this opportunity may never happen.

> "Can a woman forget her nursing child, that she should have no compassion on the son of her womb? Even these may forget, yet I will not forget you."

> (Isa. 49:15)

I used to read these verses and think the purpose was to give us a deeper understanding of God's love. It seemed as if God was saying, "Hey, it seems unlikely that a mom could forget her child. But even if she did, I won't forget you, so don't worry!" While I do think the entire Bible is a love letter, I wonder if what God is really speaking to here is our human limitations. I can't be with Ally and Bailey Grace at all times. There are moments where I'm not around, whether at school or elsewhere, that they might be left unnoticed out of their inability to add words or certain actions to particular situations. I may not forget them, but for all intents and purposes, I might as well have. Yet God. He doesn't just see all; He is Immanuel, God with us (Isa. 7:14, Matt. 1:23). He is our ever-present Help (Ps. 46:1). Nothing can separate us from Him (Rom. 8:38–39). In the highest of highs and the lowest of lows, He goes with us (Isa. 43:2).

When Bailey Grace and Ally first began having seizures, it was thought (still is) that they seize several times throughout the night. In the beginning, I was determined I would be there every single time it happened. The more I watched the monitor, the more I realized that if that was going to happen, I was not going to be doing much sleeping. After wearing myself out for a few weeks, I had to surrender the middle of the night shift to the One who never slumbers or sleeps. My mama heart wanted to be there, yet my flesh was too weak to make it a constant reality. These days, Hugh and I go to the girls' bedsides for every seizure that happens while we are still awake and then we have to trust that God Himself is there for the moments that we are not. I have to choose to believe that even when I am not present, He is. Even when I cannot speak words of truth and life over Ally and Bailey Grace, God Himself is "in (their) midst, a mighty one who will save; He will rejoice over (them) with gladness; He will quiet (them) by His love (Zeph. 3:17). These same truths that apply to the middle of the night apply on any given day at any given moment as well. Friends, we cannot be there for one another in all the ways that we wish. As a parent, we will absolutely wear ourselves out if we attempt to protect our little ones from any and every difficulty that comes their way. Beyond that, do we trust that—

> "It is good for me that I was afflicted, that I might learn your statutes."

(Ps. 119:71)

Think about your own life. When I look back, many of the trials and tribulations God allowed are the very same things that helped me truly believe my own identity and security and satisfaction in Christ. Many of the things that brought me the lowest were the very things that brought me to my knees and to my Savior. Could it be that we are falsely attempting to protect our loved ones from the very things that could bring them the ultimate peace and assurance?

Today, Ally and Bailey Grace are at school. They attend a school where I feel they get the utmost care and attention from teachers and therapists. The staff goes out of their way to make it an inclusive environment. Yet I don't know how noticed or understood the girls are in any given moment. I don't know if the other kids have genuinely enjoyed having Ally and Bailey Grace there and if they have learned to appreciate their value and worth for what it truly is. Yet this I call to mind and therefore I hope,

> "…He has said, 'I will never leave you nor forsake you.'"

(Heb. 13:5)

Even more, a day is coming in which, "Behold, at that time I (God) am going to deal with all your oppressors; I will save the lame and gather the scattered, and I will turn their shame into praise and renown in every land" (where they have suffered) (Zeph. 3:19).

Nothing is wasted in God's glorious kingdom. This thing— whatever it may be—is going to be used for His glory and your good. His promises are a resounding, never-ending, faithful yes in Christ (2 Cor. 1:20). Oh, how He sees us. Oh, how He stays forever with us. Oh, how He loves us. To Him be all the honor forever and ever.

21

A GOOD, GOOD FATHER

It's the middle of cold and flu season. This tends to be relevant in our house on multiple levels, yet this year we have thus far stayed oddly well. It is a peculiar thing to have kids who don't come with a rule book. I realize none of them do, really. However, when you go from having a year where pretty much every respiratory illness lands you in the hospital to a year where, so far, we have only had one cold, and it was relatively simple, there is a weird tension between "Have we started a new normal?" and "Don't put your guard down; don't get your hopes up."

On Sunday, we are blessed to have a "buddy system" at church for family members with special needs. For the first couple of years that the girls had a buddy, they stayed in a separate classroom away from the other kids while Hugh and I went to worship. Without getting on a completely different soapbox, if you are a caregiver to someone who has special needs, and you are married, you desperately need to find a way to participate in regular worship with one another. People always ask how Hugh and I keep our marriage together in the midst of taking care of twins who are medically fragile, and one of the main ways we continue to be able to stay connected is through regular worship together at our local church. In an age where technology is vast and podcasts are abundant, it would be so much easier to not take the time to invest in our church. Yet, there is something so profound about being able to sit with the Body of Christ, side by side, and bring our own mess to the mix. There are definitely God-given healing properties that are graced just by showing up. I also know with all my heart that the church needs to not only see but also be around Ally and Bailey Grace. The impact that their contentment and joy brings to the table is unique, and we would be doing the church an injustice if we did not allow them to participate in Bailey Grace and Ally's lives. Soapbox over. As I said, for the first two years, the girls were intentionally isolated in a classroom where germs didn't abound and where they could be cared for while Hugh and I were spiritually fed. The past two weeks, we have agreed to have the girls go to the large children's group. They sing praise songs together—one of the girls' most favorite things on any given day—and then there is a short lesson. When the idea to include Bailey Grace and Ally was presented to me, I knew without a doubt what the girls would want to do. They love being around other kids, they enjoy music so very much, and people-watching is one of their most prized hobbies. When I went to pick them up last Sunday, the excitement on their face was obvious. The buddies raved on and on about how much fun they had. They said that, in particular, the girls had loved singing, "Good, Good Father." For a moment, all my hesitations about snotty-nosed kids and germs and things that aren't in my control fell to the background, and I knew with all my heart that allowing the girls to do what their peers were doing in the church was the absolute right decision.

Flash-forward to last night.

Right before Ally went to bed, the sneezing began. Within a couple of hours of laying them down, I heard a gag, and I knew: there was some sort of respiratory virus about to begin. We were up some of the night with what appears at this point to be "just a cold" (which is never really just a cold around here). Because she doesn't have a fever, and her teachers are comfortable having her come to school to see how she does (and because they are so considerate, I believe to give me a few hours of calm before what could be a storm. They love our family so well). Mornings around here are hectic at baseline. Between getting the girls up, getting them dressed, venting their feeding tubes and giving medicines, getting them fed, brushing teeth and hair (which is always a production), and getting them into the car, I am usually out of breath by the time everyone is ready and in their car seats. (I am also usually basically in my pajamas. Priorities, people, priorities). We live less than five minutes from the school, which gives me enough time to pray for the day and whatever prayer requests are on my heart before turning up the music and listening to part of a song or two. This morning, as I turned up the radio, I had to laugh at what was playing.

Good, good Father.

The irony didn't escape me as I thought about the fact that Ally's enjoyment of that song with her peers might have been the very same moments that landed us with this illness. I pulled down the mirror to look at the girls, only to see Ally doing something that convicted my heart—really, my mind—in all the right ways.

Clapping.
She was clapping.

The beauty of her actions in this moment made it clear to me that her current sickness was having zero effect on her praise of God, of who He is, and all His promises to us. As the artist belted out, "You're a good, good Father; it's who you are," Ally clapped and waved her hands excitedly as if to communicate, "Yes, yes, you are, God!" How humbling it is to learn lesson after lesson from my seemingly intellec- tually disabled, nonverbal children. I got them out of the car and into the school just in time to hear the end of the song, and as I listened, I belted out the words, "You are perfect in *all* of Your ways. You are perfect in *all* of Your ways. You are perfect in *all* of Your ways to us."

In Matthew, chapter 18, verses 2–4, the disciples came to Jesus and asked Him who was the greatest in the kingdom of heaven. Jesus's response?

> "And calling to Him a child, He put him in the midst
> of them and said, 'Truly, I say to you, unless you turn
> and become like children, you will never enter the
> kingdom of heaven. Whoever humbles himself like
> this child is the greatest in the kingdom of heaven.'"

I do not know how much complex thinking Ally (or Bailey Grace) has the ability to do. I'm not sure if Ally comprehends that a really snotty nose might equal a hard few days. I'm not even positive she connected the fact that she had sung that same song at church on Sunday. Nevertheless, what I do know is this: her praise and trust in her heavenly Father was pleasing to Him. Her example of not allowing circumstance or "what if" to take over her rejoicing in her Daddy was worth imitating. Her ability to not let the hard things take away her worship was both admirable and biblical. I think there are things that we do naturally as children that we would be wise to implement again as adults. Ally's example this morning was a clear reminder that God "chooses what is weak in the world to shame the strong" (1 Cor. 1:27).

As I have been typing this, I received a text from the girls' teacher that Ally's symptoms are picking up a bit. I'm not sure what the next few days will hold. I can't predict what type of illness this is or if we will end up at Children's because of it. Yet, what I do know trumps the things that I do not, or, rather, Whom I do know gives me peace for the moments that everything else is unknown. We can have certain peace in the midst of all things uncertain because we have a good, good Father who already accomplished that which truly matters. We can trust His love for us as we behold both the ultimate display of love on the cross and also find perfect assurance by His power made obvious by His resurrection. Friends, we don't have to know what's coming next. We can rest in the passenger seat of our own lives when we know that our Driver is the Perfect, all-knowing, all-seeing, all-sovereign, All-Loving God over all the universe. May we clap at this reality with every twist and turn, even the most unexpected ones, with the utmost confidence in who our Daddy is.

> "He knows the way I take; when He has tried me, I shall come forth as gold."

(Job 23:10)

22

THY WILL BE DONE

Growing up, we recited it every week, this Lord's Prayer. I had read why since I was a little girl. Jesus Himself gave it as an example to how we are to pray, so pray we did. This is what He said:

> "Pray then like this:

> 'Our Father in heaven, hallowed be Your name. Your kingdom come, Your will be done, on earth as it is in heaven. Give us this day our daily bread, and forgive us our debts, as we also have forgiven our debtors. And lead us not into temptation, but deliver us from evil.'"

> (Matt. 6:9–13)

I always focused on two specific parts: give us our daily bread and lead us not into temptation. My very spiritual reason for this was that I loved to eat, and I kept falling into temptation. I figured if I asked God for both food and the ability to be good that I had pretty much covered it. I never really paid much attention to the "Your will be done" part until I was much older.

As I have said before, after the girls were born, many of my Sunday-school answers were pretty much wrecked. The love of a mama is fierce, and when both of your babies are diagnosed with a rare, life-threatening illness, you suddenly cannot simply recite words that don't make sense in your heart. While I was no longer attending a church that read the Lord's Prayer every Sunday, I was in God's Word enough to hear the sentiments of this prayer fairly often. In the beginning years of the girls' lives, I was suddenly keenly aware of all the times people used the phrase, "Your will be done." I found myself sheepishly yet honestly not able to pray those words. God's will began to feel very, very scary as we continued to pray for answers and healing and finding neither. I started to wonder what we were even saying. Why did we want God's will? Was it really able to be trusted when it seemed that so much brokenness and heaviness still abounded? Was all the evil and hard and suffering—was that God's will?

Let's get some context on the first time Jesus shared this prayer. The disciples don't seem to be picking up on the clues just yet, but Jesus is nearing the time of crucifixion. Something we have to remember about Jesus is that He is the definition of practicing what you preach. He never exhorted anyone to do anything He wasn't able and willing and already actively following through on. He was also fully God, fully man, so at that point, He already knew the exact will of the Father because He and the Father are/were one. He also was perfectly aware that that very will would lead Him down the road of Calvary to suffer and die for sins He never committed. This prayer was not just a bunch of careless words tied together for Jesus; it wasn't just a bunch of suggestions for how to live a good life. The magnitude of Jesus's purpose on earth never once left His mind, and I can imagine that as the days crept closer and closer to His death and resurrection, Jesus wanted to be both clear and tactful in His parting wisdom. His intentionality is surpassed by no other. When we think about the fact that God Himself gave us clear words for how best to please Him in our connection to Him, it should make us want to pay more attention to the heart behind each and every bit of guidance provided. That being said, when Jesus shared the Lord's Prayer, He also knew that some short time later He would be praying pieces of it in the Garden of Gethsemane.

> "And going a little farther He fell on His face and prayed, saying, 'My Father, if it be possible, let this cup pass from me; nevertheless, not as I will, but as You will.'"

(Matt. 26:39)

And again:

> "Again, for the second time, He went away and prayed, 'My Father, if this cannot pass unless I drink it, Your will be done'"

(verse 42).

And once more:

> "So leaving them again, He went away and prayed for the third time, saying the same words again."

(verse 44).

Over and over and over, Jesus talked with the Father
about what He already knew was about to go down;
yet, He always ended it with, "Not my will but Yours."
Why was that?
Was it because He knew it was the right thing to say?
Was it to prove a point to the disciples that it was the
appropriate way to pray?
Did he just tag it on for extra points?

93

The answer to all the above is absolutely not. I believe that Jesus said these words because He knew that they had power. In the midst of humbling Himself for the sake of man, He also knew with full certainty that the Father's will would always bring ultimate pleasure and perfect satisfaction.

During this same season that I was having a difficult time praying the words, "Thy will be done," God brought to mind a Psalm that has been instrumental in both my confidence in God and His plans and also my joy.

Psalm 16:

Preserve me, O God, for in You I take refuge. I say to the Lord, "You are my Lord; I have no good apart from You." As for the saints in the land, they are the excellent ones, in whom is all my delight. The sorrows of those who run after another god shall multiply; their drink offerings of blood I will not pour out or take their names on my lips. The Lord is my chosen portion and my cup; You hold my lot. The lines have fallen for me in pleasant places; indeed, I have a beautiful inheritance. I bless the Lord who gives me counsel; in the night also my heart instructs me. I have set the Lord always before me; because He is at my right hand, I shall not be shaken. Therefore my heart is glad, and my whole being rejoices; my flesh also dwells secure. For You will not abandon my soul to Sheol, or let Your holy one see corruption. You make known to me the path of life; in Your presence there is fullness of joy; at Your right hand are pleasures forevermore.

The day you begin to take God up on the fulfillment of His promises is that day that true faith begins to blossom, and this Psalm alone is chockfull of the glorious delights of intimacy with the Father. There is a far cry difference in saying you believe in God and then calling Him Lord of your life. Trusting that He is Lord means I continue to take steps toward a faith that says He is in control of all things. It means that I don't run after other things to satisfy because I know that only He is able to fully meet all my needs. When I look to God

Almighty as both my Refuge and my Portion, regardless of circumstance, my heart can remain steadfast, not because of anything I am but because of everything He is. It is one thing to claim belief in God and who He says He is with your mouth, yet what is truly in our hearts will always surface by the way we live our life and by the confidence we have in praying, "Thy will be done." You see, when I was a little girl, I think I thought that phrase was simply something we were supposed to say. I didn't experience joy in the will of God because I didn't know exactly what that will was going to bring about. Yet, as I have studied God's Word and seen the realest reality that whatever God wills is absolutely leading those who claim Him as Lord to the utmost pleasures and satisfaction, I have started to be able to pray these words both fervently and passionately. Instead of a monotone tag-on, it has been my life's joy.

I don't know if any of this is resonating with you. If you are reading this, I have a feeling that you have been in a situation where someone (maybe yourself?) asked for prayer in a certain direction and then quickly mumbled, "But only if He wills, of course." My prayer for us today is that this phrase wouldn't be an addition to our prayers but the very heart of them. God knows what He is doing. God knows what He is doing. God, my friend, knows what He is doing. When we don't know the outcome of a circumstance, He has already seen it. When we aren't sure how an illness or adoption or pregnancy or relationship or job or financial decision is going to turn out: His will is already playing out for His glory and our good. May we rest and find comfort in what God is doing today and always, for "…no eye has seen, nor ear heard, what God has prepared for those who love Him" (1 Cor. 2:9).

Thy will be done, Lord. Thy will be done!

23

TOO MANY PLATES

The girls have been getting over a seemingly mild cold. The word mild does not tend to make its appearance around here, and I have been on edge just waiting for the congestion to prove me otherwise. We have been up a few times in the night but nothing outside of normal parenting duties, really. On Friday, Ally had to be picked up one hour prior to normal carpool time for a longer coughing spell, but, really, there hasn't been anything extremely outside of what typical kids might do. It feels weird. Like a television show that ends in the middle of a scene, I keep waiting on something else to happen.

Hugh was off work yesterday. It was a Monday, so after giving the girls a bolus after school, we decided to go to the Botanical Gardens to get some fresh air. This winter has been full of weather extremes; one second it's like spring, the next it's in the teens. This particular day was milder with just a touch of cold air attached to the breeze. Hugh and I pushed the girls and talked about a number of things as we passed by somewhat barren brown grassy areas. While the gardens didn't have all the plants of spring in full array, there was a sense of creation in all the trees and somewhat half-alive blooms. Each passing section seemed to say, "Just wait a little longer. Warmer weather is coming."

My mama-bear radar is pretty much constantly set on high alert, so when Bailey Grace began behaving in some not typical ways, I was partially listening to Hugh and partially waiting for whatever was about to happen. Even though I could only see the back of her head from the angle I was placed at, as I saw her body slump forward a little and looked down at her hands, I knew she was seizing. Her fists were clenched up and held at the center of her body; her head and eyes darted back and forth. We stopped moving; and Hugh and I leaned down and began talking to her and letting her know we were right there. It's what we always do. What other options are there, really?

Bailey Grace is currently in a season where daytime seizures tend to mean only one thing: illness. It took her about twenty minutes—yes, twenty—to fully come out of the episode. Now, all the protocol will tell you five minutes in you should be giving an emergency medicine. If we gave her an emergency medicine every time we got five minutes in, we would be giving her that medicine almost every single day. The reality is, while seizures seem to hold her body and brain hostage for minutes at a time, they don't usually reach a place where we feel like we are in a crisis. Do they do long-term damage on her? Who knows. My guess is probably that subtly, yes they do. Yet, when you are in a rare category where no one on this side of heaven really knows what exactly is going on, you really only have the option to pray and do what you think is best (in our case, times two). Once Bailey Grace seemed like she was starting to feel like herself again, we continued our walk, attempting to pick up in conversation where we left off.

Last night was a relatively typical night at our house: one vomit, three more seizures split between the girls, and a couple of middle-of-the-night wake-ups. This morning, Bailey Grace had another seizure as I carried her down the stairs. I took her temperature just to ensure she wasn't febrile, then started the process of medications and feeding for the day. Both girls continued to seem just a little congested. They ate decently fine, took their boluses well, and off to school they went. While driving the very short drive to school, I had to wonder whether or not this was continued symptoms from the small cold Ally had last week; or the beginning of something new.

Several kids at school had cold-like symptoms. Did they have the same virus as the girls or something different? If they caught it, would their immune symptoms already be down enough for this on to cause bigger issues? Should I have listened to their chests this morning to make sure I didn't hear anything suspicious? I looked in the back seat and a part of me felt a little crazy. They were both smiling and singing/babbling to the music. They looked absolutely normal. But what if subconsciously something else was going on?

Bailey Grace's diaper was completely dry when we left the house. Five minutes later, when we arrived at the school, she had completely soaked through her pants. I gave the teachers an "I'm sorry" exasperated look before putting her in her wheelchair and kissing her good-bye. Because I had no answers for the teachers as far as why Bailey Grace had been seizing more, I simply told them to call me if it kept happening or if anything unusual came up. I looked down at my phone and noticed I had several texts from friends who needed responding to and one missed call. If I'm honest, instead of this making me feel loved, I simply felt overwhelmed. The reality is that even if someone has your favorite dessert in their hands waiting to give to you, if you are already balancing what feels like way too many plates, even dessert feels like just too much to add on.

Do you ever feel that way? Do you ever feel like you are holding a tray full of plates, attempting to balance everything? Sometimes it seems as if one little utensil falls off, the whole thing is going to topple over. On those days, my irritability can get to an all-time high. It seems as if everyone around me is trying to hand me another something to add to the tray when all I want to say—or really scream is, "Can't you see that there are too many plates already?"

> "Come to me, all who labor and are heavy laden, and I
> will give you rest."

> (Matt. 11:28)

I always find it interesting that Jesus speaks these words to the people right after He thanks the Father for revealing truth not to the wise of the world but to the little children. From my point of view, Bailey Grace and Ally appear very heavy-laden. They go through things multiple times a day that are painful to watch. Yet, the irony is that they don't appear to be weighted down at all. In fact, I would say the opposite is true. The girls have such a light-hearted, carefree mentality about each and every day—regardless of the circumstances. I don't think this is coincidence, either.

The truth is, Ally and Bailey Grace don't attempt to carry the plates on their own—they know they can't. They look to whoever is in front of them with utmost trust that we are going to do whatever we can to make sure they are not alone in whatever they are going through. They are humble enough to see that the things in front of them are not theirs to shoulder, and I think it's this very attitude that gives them emotional rest in whatever is going on at any given moment.

Here's some not so irony for you: in the midst of writing this chapter, I looked up at the clock and realized I needed to get a few things done around the house. I glanced at the counter to see several items of the girls, along with some toilet paper, I needed to carry up to the guest room. I attempted to pick up every single item so as to save myself a trip and—low and behold—I dropped it all. Isn't this the very lesson God might be trying to teach us? I think many of us need to take a good look at the plates we are balancing and ask ourselves two simple questions: Do I need to set a couple of plates down in order to best hold the most important ones? And maybe even more crucial: what plates do I need to bring to the foot of the cross and leave there—plates I'm not meant to carry at all?

I made a promise to God, Hugh, and a whole congregation of people that I was going to attempt to put Hugh second in this life, right after God Himself in the hierarchy. Caring for twins with special needs who are dependent on me for absolutely everything is a 24/7 job that requires almost every ounce of my energy. Before this unique assignment, there were so many different service opportunities I saw myself involved in. Prior to Ally and Bailey Grace, my ability to be an intentional and consistently present friend was much higher than it is now. I think instead of adding more plates to my tray, sometimes I need to surrender the ones that I so desperately wish I could hold. The truth is, the people who truly love us are going to extend grace upon grace to us in the midst of the story God is writing in each of our lives. Each of us are going to walk through seasons where we just can't offer as much of ourselves to the people around us as we would like. I have come to find relief in the fact that the ones who are truly going to stick it out aren't going anywhere in those drier seasons. On another note, sometimes we need to take a longer look at what's in front of us and examine whether or not we are holding things that were never ours in the first place—the past and the future being a huge part of that. I cannot change the past; therefore, I must lay it down at the throne and trust in the grace of Jesus to cover it all. There are so many things about the future—even five minutes from now—that can leave me feeling anxious and unsure. The girls are about 40 pounds each as is. How in the world am I going to carry them, bathe them, and care for them well if and when they get older? What if they are getting a worse illness than before and I'm just not seeing it? What if something bigger is going on and they just can't express it? What if they have a bad seizure and I'm not there to help? What if what's around the corner is even harder than what's already come to pass? I can "what if" all day long, yet I must put those plates down at the cross and pick up His light and easy yoke. Friends, I think it's time we trade some of these plates for the never-changing, never-failing promises of God. It might be that we are hanging on to plates that were never ours to begin with, so much so that we don't have room on the tray for the plates that would bring us rest in the first place! He offers us His yoke in exchange for ours. His yoke is easy. His burden is light. He wants to be the place where we can come drop off the things that have crowded both our hearts and our lives and feeding us the lie that one shift or stumble or break will cause it all to crumble altogether.

I truly believe that these words are a call for each of us to examine where we feel stressed and why and to ask ourselves what God has entrusted to us to care for to the best of our abilities with His help not as a backup but as the source of all that we say and do and are. *He* is at the center of this story, not us. The pressure is off. If there are too many plates, rest assured there is a safe, competent, trustworthy place to lay those plates down. At some point, maybe we will be asked to pick them back up with the help of our gracious Savior. Regardless, we are summoned—invited really—to pick up the infinite promises of a holy God who never leaves and never forsakes. Anything He places on us is to free—never to burden. Come to the table and feast on limitless grace and love and provision. It's all there waiting for you—too many plates to count.

24

RUBBLE

"The strength of those who bear the burdens is failing. There is too much rubble. By ourselves we will not be able to rebuild the wall."

(Neh. 4:10)

Our pastor said it a few Sundays ago. We are going through the book of Nehemiah, and when we got to Chapter 4, he posed a simple question: "Do you ever feel like there's just too much rubble?"

In a matter of a few seconds, my mind wandered to the current worries of my life: seizures, both the typical ones and some new ones presenting themselves. A terrible cold and flu season in front of us with worries of "What will we catch?" in front of me. Some GI issues that have gotten more chronic for both girls. Student loans that we seem to barely chip away at month to month. Changing community. At times, lack of intimacy in our marriage. It seems like there's just not enough emotional energy to give on the hard weeks. All the waiting and what-ifs surrounding adoption. Navigating extended family relationships. Figuring out what in the world we are going to spend our time doing in the summer.

Rubble.
Rubble.
Rubble.

I love this idea of simplifying our lives. I try to do a (relatively) good job of cleaning out drawers and closets and giving away toys and stuff that we no longer use or need. Yet, what do we do when the stuff in front of us isn't stuff we can just put to the side? What do we do when there are figurative rocks and stones that need to be—that must be—acknowledged and dealt with? Most of us know the phrase "Let go and let God," but where is our personal responsibility in it all? Where do we draw the line between being still and taking action?

> "Do not be afraid of them. Remember the Lord, who
> is great and awesome, and fight for your brothers, your
> sons, your daughters, your wives, and your homes."

(Neh. 4:14b)

Remember.

I am very good at remembering, yet, often, I'm not bringing my memory back to the right thing—rather, the right One. So often, I look back and think about past fear, past pain, past trials. This verse reminds me of the power of meditating on God Himself. Christ-follower: we must, we must, we *must* seek to see God and fixate our entire being on who He is and what He says He can and will do. We have to cease marinating thoughts that do not set God in His rightful place. He is the center of this story, and until we make that our focus, everything else will be blurry and disjointed. We don't just remember. We remember the Lord Almighty and that changes everything.

> Fight for your brothers, your sons, your daughters,
> your wives, and your homes.
> Fight.

How often do we find ourselves fighting, yet fighting for the wrong thing? Friends, we are called to place aside our personal comforts and, at times, personal desires in order to fulfill our unique assignment as a member of the Body of Christ. We are called to be like Jesus—to lay down our lives for others. Moreover, who is our neighbor? Who is our family?

> "While He (Jesus) was still speaking to the people, behold, His mother and His brothers stood outside, asking to speak to Him. But He replied to the man who told Him, 'Who is my mother, and who are my brothers?' And stretching out His hand toward His disciples, He said, 'Here are my mother and my brothers! For whoever does the will of my Father in heaven is my brother and sister and mother.'"
>
> (Matt. 12:46–50)

> "And behold, a lawyer stood up to put Him to the test, saying, 'Teacher, what shall I do to inherit eternal life?' He said to him, 'What is written in the Law? How do you read it?' And he answered, 'You shall love the Lord your God with all your heart and with all your soul and with all your strength and with all your mind, and your neighbor as yourself.' And he said to him, 'You have answered correctly; do this, and you will live.' But he, desiring to justify himself, said to Jesus, 'And who is my neighbor?' Jesus replied, 'A man was going down from Jerusalem to Jericho and he fell among robbers, who

stripped him and beat him and departed, leaving him half dead. Now by chance a priest was going down that road, and when he saw him he passed by the other side. So likewise, a Levite, when he came to the place and saw him, passed by on the other side. But a Samaritan, as he journeyed, came to where he was, and when he saw him, he had compassion. He went to him and bound up his wounds, pouring on oil and wine. Then he set him on his own animal and brought him to an inn and took care of him. And the next day he took out two denarii and gave them to the innkeeper, saying, 'Take care of him, and whatever more you spend, I will repay you when I come back. Which of these three, do you think, proved to be a neighbor to the man who fell among the robbers?' He said, 'The one who showed him mercy.' And Jesus said to him, 'You go, and do likewise.'"

(Luke 10:25–37)

"'For I was hungry and you gave me food, I was thirsty and you gave me drink, I was a stranger and you welcomed me, I was naked and you clothed me, I was sick and you visited me, I was in prison and you came to me.' Then the righteous will answer him saying, 'Lord, when did we see you hungry and feed you, or thirsty and gave you drink? And when did we see you a stranger and welcome you, or naked and clothe you? And when did we see you in prison and visit you?' And the King will answer them, 'Truly, I say to you, as you did it to one of the least of these, my brothers, you did it to me.'"

(Matt. 25:35–40)

I know that was a lot to take in at once, but I'm praying that in these moments, the Lord will open the eyes of our hearts to what He's trying to say to us. I think that we spend a lot of time fighting, yet not fighting about the things that bring unity within the Church. Jesus makes it clear that the world will know that we follow Him by the way we show our love to one another (John 13:35). If we waste all our energy on focusing on our own personal rubble, how much do we have left over to truly fight for the souls and needs of our true brothers and sisters? Self can be a tricky thing. May we love our neighbors like ourselves, and may we be so focused on our God and our neighbor that our selfish tendencies do not have room to grow.

Finally, do not be afraid.

I put this one last because I think that we can find plenty reasons to fear when we have spiritual amnesia about our God and His purpose and plans. When we remember our God and when we ask Him to give us the desire, strength, and ability to fight for our true family, fear no longer has place in our lives. God tells us not to fear not because there aren't things to be afraid of but because in the midst of all those things, He is with us. If there is too much rubble in your life or mine, I want to gently ask you (ask myself!) if we are bearing burdens that were not meant to be ours. So much of the noise that is in my daily life is stuff that I can choose—that I must choose—to leave in the past or future. I must trust that God goes "before and behind" (Ps. 139:5) and that He has more than enough strength to bear it all. By ourselves, we are not able. But God. He gives us mercy for each day.

We no longer have to fear or fixate on the rubble
when we know we are a child of the Rock.
Our mountain of what seems like problems—
no matter how many or how big—turns to pebbles
in light of our Steadfast Savior.
The Rock won't move.

May we lay each and every thing at the foot of His glorious (and victorious!) throne.

> "So we do not lose heart. Though our outer self is wasting away, our inner self is being renewed day by day. For this light momentary affliction is preparing for us an eternal weight of glory beyond all comparison, as we look not to the things that are seen but to the things that are unseen. For the things that are seen are transient, but the things that are unseen are eternal."
>
> (2 Cor. 4:16–18)

25

OUR ULTIMATE WAIT

December 2015:

I sent Hugh a text that simply said this: I think I'm ready to start the adoption process.

Hugh's response?

Yes! Let's talk about it tonight.

Hugh had been opening up the conversation for a few weeks now—this idea of adding to our family. In the naïve years (you know, that first year or so of marriage when you picture the 2.5 kids and white picket fence), we had said that we wanted "several" kids, whatever that meant. When Hugh and I had been in Ethiopia, a couple of weeks before he proposed, a man on our trip had a visit with his daughter's birth mom. As he told the story at dinner that night, tears rolled down my face. Hugh's eyes were all watery as well, yet I noticed that not everyone seemed that affected by the story. Flash-forward another year to our trip to Bangladesh. While the trip itself was impactful in more ways than I could count, the few days we spent in Bangkok, Thailand, in between were monumental for us as well. At this point, Hugh and I were married, and we both fell in love with the culture. We loved the food, the chaotic yet peaceful atmosphere, and mostly the beautiful people. One morning, we sat at the guesthouse and talked about the possibility of adopting a little girl from

Thailand. We decided we would call her Lily Grace and even bought an ornament of a lily there to remind ourselves of this longing.

Back to December 2015.

Hugh was a chief resident, and I was continuing to spend a lot of time as both mom and caregiver to two girls with ever-growing, ever-changing, and never-stopping needs. I was content yet exhausted. When Hugh began to open up the conversation about adding to our family, I immediately shut it down, praying for the Lord's will being very far from my mind. I already felt overwhelmed many days. At the time, Hugh was still planning on doing a Fellowship in Pediatric Emergency Medicine (another cool God story for another time). Money was tight, and Hugh's schedule wasn't going to get any easier. I had squelched this desire for more children in the name of wisdom and decided that maybe that just wasn't in the cards for us anymore. But God. Around Christmas, I sat on the couch right by our Christmas tree, and a particular ornament caught my eye. It was the one we had bought for "Lily Grace." I have never heard the Lord audibly speak, but every now and then He speaks to my heart in a way that pierces my soul and makes me more aware of His voice. On that particular morning, I felt His still small voice whisper to my soul.

"Are you ready?"
I didn't have to ask for what. I knew exactly what He meant.

"Am I ready?" I said it out loud. "Lord, you see this home. You see my stress level. You know my husband's career path. Am I ready? Hardly not."

Silence for a few minutes, and then this: "When will you be?"

I took a deep breath. "Well, I'm not sure ever." I spoke it somewhat quietly but firmly with a touch of defiance.

His response?

"Do you feel called?"

This time, silence on my end. I knew the answer. Yes. I had felt called to adopt since before I could remember.

"Yes." This time I said nothing verbally, only whisper in my heart.

His next question changed everything.

"Then what are you waiting for?"

I thought about it for a few minutes and then knew what I had to do. I pulled the phone out, texted Hugh, and that's where our journey began.

After praying for a few days, Hugh and I knew we felt led to start the Domestic Adoption process. This surprised us both, seeing as we had a heart for other countries; also, I had worked in International Adoption, and it was more familiar. Yet we saw the need and felt the nudge, so by faith we went. After filling out loads of paperwork, we began the fundraising process. By God's grace we raised the money in a matter of months. At the time, I saw this as maybe a hint that this process would be quicker than we thought. Our particular agency is one that really puts the birth parent's needs first. The birth parent actually has the opportunity to choose who parents her child, so getting an idea of "how long" was somewhat impossible. After saying yes to a few birth mothers and having them choose other families, an opportunity came up through a canvas of details tied together that had us meeting a birth mother who was due in February 2016. We met this woman, prayed with her, and had dinner with her. She called us on Thanksgiving "just to say hi." She had been very open that she wasn't sure whether or not she was going to parent or not, but it just felt too much like the hand of God to not keep pressing forward.

At the beginning of February, Bailey Grace's seizure took a really bad turn. She began having multiple seizures throughout the day, and on February 6, 2017, we had to take her to the Emergency Room to try to figure out what in the world was going on and how to keep her as safe as we could. That very same morning, "our" birth mother—who wasn't ours, after all—had her precious little boy and chose to raise him as her own. I sat in the Emergency Room in almost disbelief. I had anticipated being at a hospital meeting our son. Instead, I was sitting in the ER watching my daughter seize uncontrollably. Why, God?

As I am writing this, it is now February 2018. We have heard no several times since then, and we continue to wait. This morning, we got word that a couple who we are waiting to hear a yes or no from are going to need more time. Today is not just February, it is February 6, exactly a year after my mama heart was broken for a child who was never meant to be my own—a child I prayed for daily, a little boy whose safety and love and knowledge of the Gospel I still pray for at times. When I realized the timing of it all, I was just sure that this was God's glorious plan. That He was going to give us a yes a year after a really hard no.

> "Wait for the Lord; be strong, and let your heart take courage; wait for the Lord!"
>
> (Ps. 27:14)

Our Make-a-Wish trip to Disney World was nothing short of marvelous. There were too many great things to say about it, but one of my favorite parts was this magical thing called the Genie Pass. At all the Disney World parks, we were given this pass that allowed us to never wait in a single line regardless of how long the wait time was. It was glorious. We would walk up to the front of the line, throw the pass up, and immediately be ushered to the Handicap Access at the front. Some of the rides would have lines all the way to the end, and a sign at the top would give an approximate wait time. Even though we didn't have to wait, I always appreciated that sign. It seemed like even if the sign said longer than you wanted to wait, at least you knew what you were getting into. Oddly enough, it's the same way I felt when we were waiting for a diagnosis for Bailey Grace and Ally. Each of the tests we ran came with an approximate wait time. Yes, the five-month test was more excruciating than the two-week tests; yet because I knew it was going to take a while, I was able to distract myself for the time being.

This morning's e-mail was painful not because it was a no but because it left us in the gray. The couple does not know how much time they are going to need to make a decision, and there were absolutely no time guidelines given. The funny thing about this chapter is that as you are reading this, you will know whether this child is ours or not. Eventually, answers will come. So why is waiting so hard? And what makes it even more challenging to wait without knowing how long you will be waiting?

> "The Lord is not slow to fulfill His promise as some count slowness, but He is patient toward you, not wishing that any should perish, but that all should reach repentance."

(2 Pet. 3:9)

The verse above? It's about the Lord's return, you know. If you are a Christian, your entire existence is one of waiting for the Lord's promise to be fulfilled. The Bible is full of verses that remind us to wait on the Lord: Psalm 37:7, Psalm 123:2, Isaiah 30:18, Jeremiah 14:22, Psalm 25:5, Psalm 145:15–16, James 5:7–8, Luke 12:35–40, 1 Corinthians 1:7, 1 Corinthians 4:5, Titus 2:13, Hebrews 9:28, Psalm 5:3, Romans 8:23, Galatians 5:5, Psalm 33:20, Psalm 130:5, Isaiah 51:5, Micah 7:7, Isaiah 8:17, Romans 8:23–25, Lamentations 3:24–26, Revelation 6:9–11, Genesis 49:18, Psalm 39:7, Mark 15:43, and Luke 2:25.

Over and over God tells us that it is Him that we are waiting on.

So maybe this is why He has us wait on all the things time and time again. Maybe this waiting isn't just about perfect timing; maybe it's teaching us to have endurance in waiting for our faith to have sight. Maybe—just maybe—the waiting has a much greater purpose than the thing we are waiting for in itself.

I'll be honest. When I have an end date to my waiting, I can distract myself pretty well up until the said waiting ends. If I don't have a timeline, however, I recognize my dependence on the Lord in the waiting in a much greater way. There is no distracting yourself when you aren't sure how long the middle part is going to last. It requires you to lean hard on the Lord and His promises in a way that instant gratification never could.

This morning as I did yoga, the instructor asked us to do a "side bind." A side bind requires you to lean to the side with one leg bent and clasp your hands together tightly underneath your legs. As I glanced up (I do online classes) to my wall, I saw the painting that held the quote, "Bind my wandering heart to thee," and I knew. That's what the waiting was doing. That's what He was inviting me to do in the wait: bind my heart and my very existence to Him, to His promises, and to His plan. It's a beautiful place to find yourself in, really; this place of having to go to the Lord over and over to be reminded that He is working, that His plans are good, and that His answers are perfect.

I do not know how long we will wait to hear from this couple, yet what I do know helps me to have courage in the midst of the things that I do not.

Even though it's hard, if it means more of You, God, I will wait.

Even though it's vulnerable, if it's stretching and increasing my faith, I will wait.

Even though I don't know the outcome, because I do know the One in control of it, I will wait.

> Without fear.
> Without stress.
> Bound only to my Father.
> You are the One we wait for, our Ultimate Wait.

26

THE ONLY THING

"Now as they went on their way, Jesus entered a village. And a woman named Martha welcomed Him into her house. And she had a sister called Mary, who sat at the Lord's feet and listened to His teaching. But Martha was distracted with much serving. And she went up to Him and said, 'Lord, do you not care that my sister has left me to serve alone? Tell her then to help me.' But the Lord answered her, 'Martha, Martha, you are anxious and troubled about many things, but one thing is necessary. Mary has chosen the good portion, which will not be taken away from her.'"

(Luke 10:38–42)

This Scripture has me feeling all kinds of annoyed—mainly because I know that I am certainly Martha in the scenario. I picture myself, knowing Jesus is in my town and desperate to spend time with Him and show Him that I care. I, like Martha, would want all the details to be as perfect as they could. I would want to cook a delicious meal for Jesus; I would take the time to light candles and diffuse all the delightful things and ensure Jesus felt right at home. Is that so wrong? After all, of course Mary is just sitting at Jesus's feet. It's not her house. If I'm Martha, I might feel bitterness or frustration begin to creep in as I watched Mary spend time with the very one I was attempting to be hospitable toward. If Mary would help out just a bit, all the things would get done quicker, and maybe we could both sit at His feet. Instead, here Martha is getting everything done that has to be done, watching her sister reap the benefits of Jesus's presence in Martha's home.

> "But seek first the Kingdom of God and His righteousness, and all these things will be added to you."
>
> (Matt. 6:33)

These days, I wake up around 5:00 AM. The house is silent, and my routine is predictable. I wash my face, get dressed, come into the kitchen, and empty the dishwasher. I get out all the girls' morning medication and feeding supplies; then I pack Hugh's lunch. Finally, I sit down for as much time as the girls and our schedule allows to read God's Word and spend time talking to Him. On the days that everyone is sleeping peacefully still, the quiet is soothing to my soul. There is something about silence that makes me feel like, for one second, things are under control.

> "God is the Blessed Controller of all things, the King over all kings and the Master of all masters."
>
> (1 Tim. 6:15)

When Mary was sitting at Jesus's feet, I wonder what she was thinking. Beyond that, what was Jesus speaking about? Often in the New Testament, we get to hear pieces of conversations that Jesus had with the people around Him. Then there are other moments—like this one—where we are not given any details on what is being spoken. However, one thing is always constant: whatever He is saying, the people's hearts are engaged and drawn to His words. Enter in Mary.

I wonder if she had intended to help Martha out with whatever needed to be done—the cooking, the cleaning, the entertaining—yet as
Jesus began speaking, there was a place in her soul that craved each
and every word, and suddenly she couldn't do anything but listen.

> "For where your treasure is, there your heart will be
> also."

(Matt. 6:21)

Jeremiah 17:9 tells us that our hearts are deceptive. The Lord reminds
us several times in His Word that only He fully knows each of our
hearts, that even we can deceive ourselves into thinking our priorities
are a certain way when they actually are another. Enter in what we
treasure. It seems to me that the things that we focus on—that we
spend our time, money, and energy on—are a very map to what our
hearts cherish.

I would like to think that because I begin most every day in God's
Word and spending time with Him, that must mean He's my number-
one priority. The problem is, once the clock hits 6:45 AM, and the
girls are out of bed, my mind and body enter in to task mode, and
suddenly I'm, as Martha was, "distracted by much serving." It all
sounds super holy until the heart is laid bare. I have read about heart
ultrasounds—how a specially trained technician uses a machine
called a cardiac sonographer to see a live picture of the heart. They
use a gel to slide a microphone device called a transducer over the
chest area, which allows reflected sound waves to provide an actual
visual of the heart itself. While this process sounds complicated, we
can be assured that the reality of God seeing our hearts is not. He
made us; all He has to do is simply look. We can fool ourselves and fool
others into thinking our serving is being done for the glory of God,

but we cannot fool God Himself. I think sometimes, like Martha, I get so obsessive with my serving that I forget to turn and rest at the feet of the One who is at the center of it all. I don't think God was telling Martha that her serving was wrong; I think He was digging in deeper to the bigger issue at stack: whose heart was turned toward Jesus in those moments?

The truth is, if I'm going to be a woman who rests in the presence of the Lord, I'm going to have to do more resting. And this doesn't necessarily mean that I'm going to be sitting still! As a wife and mom (and really just human being in general!), we have a lot of obligations and oftentimes, there just isn't a space to literally stop moving. Yet our hearts. God isn't as interested in physically slowing you down as He is in changing the posture of your heart to be one of rest. The truth is, the "one thing that is necessary" that Mary had found was a heart fixated on Jesus! Martha was so busy serving that she had forgotten the One she was serving altogether. She was making Jesus's visit to her home about performance and work instead of relationship. How easy it is for us to do this in a world full of so many distractions that pull at our heartstrings! So much of our serving is done in attempt to control the circumstance around us instead of as an act of love to the One who is in control of all.

> "She looks well to the ways of her household and does not eat the bread of idleness."
>
> (Prov. 31:27)

God isn't asking us to stop our labor. He doesn't want us to throw away the to-do lists; I think maybe He's just gently exhorting us to add some things to them. I believe God would rather me do three things in love, with a pure heart, than twenty of them out of obligation or fear. I think that He is well pleased when I keep my mind set on His glory in the midst of the day-to-day rather than rushing around trying to accomplish more than He has required. Today, I challenge us to ask ourselves what He wants us to do. I think we need to take a good look at what's in front of us and ask ourselves how we can do these things well, to the glory of God, instead of trying to do "all the things" to the glory of self. Regardless of how many things we "have" to do today, might we remember that in Christ, we already have the one thing that is needed: God Himself! In Christ, we are free to live and love and serve and work with joy that He Himself provides. May we have more of a Mary heart in the midst of every task before us. And,

> "whatever you do, work heartily, as for the Lord and not for men, knowing that from the Lord you will receive the inheritance as your reward. You are serving the Lord Christ."

(Col. 3:23–24)

To Him be the glory forever.

27

FORGIVEN MUCH

"One of the Pharisees asked Him to eat with him, and He went into the Pharisee's house and reclined at the table. And behold, a woman of the city, who was a sinner, when she learned that He was reclining at the table in the Pharisee's house, brought an alabaster flask of ointment, and standing behind Him at His feet, weeping, she began to wet His feet with her tears and wiped them with the hair of her head and kissed His feet and anointed them with the ointment. Now when the Pharisee who had invited Him saw this, he said to himself, 'If this man were a prophet He would have known who and what sort of woman this is that is touching Him, for she is a sinner.' And Jesus answering said to him, 'Simon, I have something to say to you.' And he answered, 'Say it, Teacher.'"

(Luke 7:36–40)

"'A certain moneylender had two debtors. One owed five hundred denarii, and the other fifty. When they could not pay, he cancelled the debt of both. Now which of them will love him more?' Simon answered, 'The one, I suppose, for whom he cancelled the larger debt.' And He said to him,

'You have judged rightly.' Then turning toward the woman he said to Simon, 'Do you see this woman? I entered your house; you gave me no water for my feet, but she has wet my feet with her tears and wiped them with her hair. You gave me no kiss, but from the time I came in she has not ceased to kiss my feet. You do not anoint my head with oil, but she has anointed my feet with ointment. Therefore, I tell you, her sins, which are many, are forgiven—for she loved much. But he who is forgiven little, love little.'"

(Luke 7:41–47)

The Pharisee above and Martha in the chapter before seem to have a lot in common. They both get super disgruntled when they see someone else getting attention from Jesus when they feel like the person doesn't deserve it. In this particular story, Jesus has once again entered into someone's home to simply be with them. It doesn't say who else was there, but we know that there were others at the table watching this interaction. Who knows how the woman—simply called "the sinful woman"—knew that Jesus was there, but when she found out, she knew she had to go. A lump rises in my throat to think about the bravery required of her to do this. After all, if her sins were at all adulterous, women like her were stoned and killed by men like the Pharisees. She didn't just show up at the market; she walked into the house of the very one who could end her life!

I wonder what made the first tear appear. Maybe it was the shame she felt. Maybe it was the love she was experiencing just being in Jesus's presence. Maybe it was simply the opportunity to be at His feet. Either way, once the tears began, she just couldn't stop them. Embarrassed maybe, she wiped Jesus's feet with the only thing she had—her own hair. This One—the One who knew the very number of hairs on her head, the God who kept all her tears in a bottle—she was in His very presence, and it was just too much for her fragile heart to handle.

The Pharisees were always looking for an opportunity to throw Jesus under the bus, to discount what His followers were saying about Him. Jesus, knowing each of their thoughts, knew what Simon was thinking. Simon was sure that if Jesus knew this woman's reputation, He wouldn't be a stone's throw away from her, much less allowing her to anoint His feet with expensive oils. Jesus was never afraid to call out someone's thoughts in order to reach another layer of their heart, so Jesus went on to tell this Pharisee that while He did in fact know everything this woman had done (or would ever do!), He was much more interested in her heart than her sins (maybe because He knew that He was going to put those to death soon enough?)

I used to think that the next part, the verse that says, "…he who is forgiven little, loves little" (verse 45), was talking about the amount of sins. By implication, this woman was most likely an adulteress. So obviously she was more sinful than the Pharisee, right?

I'm not so sure.

Jesus was always getting on to the Pharisees for cleaning the outside of the cup instead of the inside (Matt. 23:25). He wasn't as interested in calling out those who supposedly didn't have their acts together as he was in calling out those who wouldn't admit that they didn't. As I read these verses, I wonder if this "forgiven little" is less about a tally of sins and more about our heart's belief in the forgiveness offered through Christ alone. The truth is, it doesn't matter what my list of good deeds are—all are rags in comparison to the holiness of Christ (Isa. 64:6). Moreover, when we get to heaven, our list of sins won't be what determines whether or not we enter into heaven. Our response at the heavenly gates will simply be one name: Jesus. He is our righteousness! He is our answer no matter how long or short our list of wrongs may be.

Maybe we can only love much when we truly believe that all our sins have been forgiven.

Maybe we can preach righteousness in Christ until our faces turn blue, but if we haven't fully trusted in Him to make our slate clean, we haven't accepted that we have been forgiven much in the first place. Maybe we love much by simply knowing we really have been forgiven—fully and completely. Maybe it's our acceptance of this truth that makes our cups runneth over with love—not the length of our lists of rights or wrongs.

Jesus didn't just stop there. He looked at the woman and said to her, "Your sins are forgiven." And as if that wasn't enough, he said to her, "Your faith has saved you; go in peace" (verse 50). I'm not sure; but I doubt this woman—known as sinful—had been told to go in peace in quite some time. Isn't that just like our God to allow us to sit and cry at His feet and then equip us to step forward in the very faith He gives? I don't know what this woman had planned for the rest of the day, but I have a feeling that whatever she did, she did with a lot less weight on her shoulders. Being in the presence of the Almighty strengthens us to walk in confidence and faith in the One whose opinion of us isn't turned by circumstance or season. When we have an Audience of One, we are able to go forward in faith, our identity secure in who He is and who He says we are.

Friend, do you know that you have been forgiven much?

If you find yourself not loving much, maybe that question is a good place to start. Our God went to the greatest lengths of all time to insure we knew His love for us. He came down and was nailed to a cross that He didn't deserve but willingly submitted to in order to display the love that He has had for us since before the beginning of time. He died and was resurrected to prove to us that He has power over all things. He lives to intercede for us whenever our hearts, our fellow human beings, or our Enemy himself accuses us. If we are in

Christ, our books are written in the Book of Life, and our eternity is sealed secure with Him forever, starting right now. The past is the past, and the future is sure—always with Him.

> Let's press into our forgiveness in order to love more
>   fully.
> He who promised is faithful

(Heb. 10:23).

28

THE PROBLEM WITH FAITH

He's not our son.

T he one I talked about a few chapters ago? He's not it. This is what I wrote in my prayer journal yesterday morning:
God, you have a plan. Hope deferred makes the heart sick. Father, I confess I'm weary in the waiting for the adoption. Weary in nos and time passed. I know you will strengthen us for the journey; I pray for continued trust as we patiently wait for answers from You. I pray this is our son! You are able, and You already know; therefore, we come to You boldly, and I ask you to overcome my unbelief and pride in it all. You are working.

By the afternoon, we received the e-mail that the birth couple had chosen another family, that as they looked through profiles, one family continued to stick out, and they just knew. We had prayed for this—prayed for clarity for this brave couple—we just had hoped it was us they would be leaning toward. When you get two years in, and you can barely count the number of "not yets" on both hands, you begin to physically feel the fight to believe God is going to work. All throughout the remainder of the day, I literally had tightness in my chest that was laboring to trust that God is who He says He is. Suffering is a funny thing; in that, it tightropes between strengthening and weakening your faith, all at the same time.

"And we know that for those who love God all things work together for good, for those who are called according to His purpose."

(Rom. 8:28)

Do I love God?

This is a question I ask myself almost daily. After Jesus walked the road of Calvary, was buried and then raised, He appeared to the disciples again on an afternoon when they were fishing. The scenario almost seems like déjà vu in ways. They haven't caught any fish, and then Jesus appears and gives them advice on where to throw the net. They don't recognize Him as who He is yet still; they heed his suggestion, and suddenly they have more fish than their nets can contain. It is in this moment that Simon Peter recognizes Jesus as Himself. Simon Peter literally puts his outer garment back on and jumps into the sea to get to His Lord. When he gets to the land, Jesus has already built a fire, fish already being prepared, yet still He asks Peter to bring some of the fish that they just caught. Simon Peter brings as many as he can haul back up to Jesus, and they all sat and ate breakfast together.

Keeping in mind the reality that right before Jesus's death, Peter had denied Him three times (just like Jesus had told him he would). This is the interaction between the two of them once breakfast was finished:

"...Jesus said to Simon Peter, 'Simon, son of John, do you love Me more than these (others do—with total commitment and devotion?).' He said to Him, 'Yes, Lord, You know that I love You (with a deep, personal affection, as for a close friend).' Jesus said to him, 'Feed my lambs.' Again He said to him a second time, 'Simon, son of John, do you love Me (with total commitment and devotion?)' He said to Him, 'Yes, Lord, You know that I love You (with a deep, personal affection,

125

as for a close friend).' Jesus said to him, 'Shepherd my sheep.' He said to him a third time, 'Simon, son of John, do you love Me (with a deep personal affection for me, as for a close friend?)' And he said to Him, 'Lord, You know everything; You know that I love You (with a deep, personal affection, as for a close friend).' Jesus said to him, 'Feed my sheep.'"

(John 21:15–17, Amplified Version)

I used to read this and think that this was Jesus really leaning into the command for Peter to shepherd the people God had entrusted to him, but now I'm not so sure there isn't a deeper meaning. It seems that Jesus was giving Peter the opportunity to heal the wound that he created whenever he denied Jesus prior to Jesus's death. Everything the Lord does is intentional, and it's no mistake that Jesus asked Simon Peter this question three times in a row—as many times as Peter denied him. When I read verses like this, I am reminded of the ever-fierce compassion that God has for us. He is so full of mercy, so much so that He calls someone "the disciple whom I love" that He knew was going to publicly deny Him in His greatest moment of need.

When I think about the love of God in the midst of our frail humanity, I can't help but be assured that, yes, by the grace of God, I do, in fact, love Him. I don't love Him perfectly—only He is able to do that. I falter in my allegiance to Him based on circumstance and emotion. Truth be told, my faith is actually pretty weak. Yet, God tells me that faith the size of a mustard seed is indeed faith that can do big things—things like moving mountains (Matt. 17:20). He also reminds me over and over in His Word to hold on to hope.

"So now faith, hope, and love abide, these three; but the greatest of these is love."

(1 Cor. 13:13)

Why does love trump faith and hope?
If faith and hope are so important, then why does
love end up on top?

"For now we see in a mirror dimly, but then face to
face. Now I know in part; then I shall know fully, even
as I have been fully known."

(1 Cor. 13:12)

There lies our answer.

The only problem with faith is that one day, it won't be needed. One day, our faith will be sight! If faith is "the assurance of things hoped for, the conviction of things unseen" (Heb. 11:1), then we can hold on to the reality that there will be a day when faith and hope will no longer be needed, for we will be with Him forever!

When I think about the fact that this isn't our son, it makes me sad. When I let my mind marinate on how long we have been waiting and not knowing how much longer we have to wait, I can feel heartsick. Yet, if I fixate on the promises of God, on Jesus as a "sure and steadfast anchor of my soul," a hope that very well enters into the inner place behind the curtain (Heb. 6:19), I am assured that ultimately, God knows exactly what He is doing. I am able to love Him because He first loved me (1 John 4:19). It's not that faith and hope aren't crucial to our journey on earth; it's just that when we finally reach the end of this journey, they will no longer be needed, yet Love Himself will still remain.

I e-mailed our social worker back, thanked her for answers, texted Hugh to let him know, took a deep breath, and then, do you know what I did? I worshipped. By the grace of God, I turned on some praise songs, I raised my hands, and I worshipped. A far cry from my response this time a year ago, where tears and whys overtook any other response.

He is changing me.
He is working.

Only He has the power to give our faith and our hope eyes to see the one day, and by the time we get to heaven, yesterday will always be gone.

All glory to the One who never fails us. May we have faith and hope to believe that Love will always remain.

To Him be the glory, forever and ever.

29

WEAK

Many of us have read it.

Paul himself said that not only was he learning to be "content with weaknesses" but also that he was choosing to "boast all the more gladly of his weaknesses" (2 Cor. 12, pieces of verses 9–10). In certain seasons of my life in which I was allowing my flesh to dictate basically every step that my body, mind, and emotions took, I found great comfort in this and looked at it as an excuse to sin because, after all, my weaknesses showed God's power, right? There was a part of me that knew—really knew—that Paul meant much more by these truths than just a cop-out to keep falling into sin, but at the time, my pride talked me into thinking that my greatest weaknesses were the areas that I struggled to hand over to God. In ways, I equated weakness with worldly living. While I think there are partial truths in this, I believe there is a distinction in conscious sins and personal limitations. Let me explain.

I have mentioned before that February–May of 2017 felt like a whirlwind of one crisis after another. I truly think I ran on adrenaline for three months straight—or, more than that, I think God just carried us from one wave to the next. Years ago, in the trenches of the beginning of the hard and unknown with our girls, I decided with fervor that I would rather ride the waves out being carried by the Lord and then stand on the shore with an umbrella drink in my hand. What I mean by that is that walking through deep suffering with the Lord being the only One capable of being all-knowing and all-comforting and all-powerful gave me a deep sense of the reality that, as Philippians 3:10 tells us, "sharing in His sufferings" is not an option for the Christian but a given. God has ushered me into a level of intimacy with Himself that satisfies my soul even in the midst of lions—sometimes, most especially in the midst of them. I think in those beginning stages, it had to be so very obvious that only God Himself could give Hugh and me the heart posture of peace in all that we were going through. I truly believe that even those of you who may not be sure what you believe about Christ can see His presence permeating the details of the story He is writing in our family—to the glory of His name and never ours. Back when Hugh was a resident, there were times where he would be on a 30-hour PICU call (which really meant about 40 hours of single parenting), where God would make Nehemiah 8:10 a crystal-clear reality for me: the joy of the Lord was my strength. Not just in word but also in actuality. The girls and I would go to hard doctor's appointments and be told heart-breaking things, only to come home to therapies and unknown night patterns and feeding difficulties, yet He took on the weight of it all so firmly that the yoke truly felt light. There were days, of course, that the burden felt like too much to bear. On those days, He would remind me that I was trying to pick something up that wasn't mine to carry. He would gently yet powerfully open my stubborn hands and take away the load, always replacing it with His peace.

This is the kind of weakness I'm speaking about.

"...and let the one who is thirsty come; let the one who desires take the water of life without price."

(Rev. 22:17b)

Have you ever woken up in the middle of the night with your mouth so dry that you almost feel like you have to have a drink in order to be able to go back to sleep? I am a creature of habit, and I always keep a bottle of water beside my bed. Some nights, that bottle goes untouched. Every now and then (often if I have had a lot of salt the night before) I will wake up so thirsty that I chug the entire thing at once. I always take it as a way of my body telling me that it needs to be filled.

When the girls are hydrated well, blood work is usually a quick and easy process. When they are dehydrated, however, it can take several sticks before the nurse is able to get a vein to "work." They say this is because the veins shrink whenever they don't have as much moisture. Veins are important because they carry blood throughout the different systems of the body (my non-medical background synopsis), but it's not really the veins themselves that are necessary so much as what's inside them.

> "But we have this treasure in jars of clay, to show that
> the surpassing power belongs to God and not to us."

> (2 Cor. 4:7–9)

> The thirstier (or hungrier) we are, the more likely we
> are to look for something to drink (or eat).

> "Why do you spend your money for that which is not
> bread, and your labor for that which does not satisfy?
> Listen diligently to me, and eat what is good, and
> delight yourselves in rich food."

> (Isa. 55:2)

When we are in a place where food and drink abound, it's much harder to make choices that will actually nourish our bodies. I tend to enjoy healthier foods (or, rather, the way those foods make me feel), but when I'm at a breakfast buffet, I have a hard time choosing oatmeal over a cinnamon roll. It's not that the pastries are bad in themselves; it's just that at the end of the day, what we truly need is that which will fuel us and fill us up.

When we were in Bangladesh, we spent one evening with a group of elementary-aged boys who were orphans living under the care of some of the Christ followers in the village. We took them to a restaurant (something almost none of them had experienced), and my observations of the boy who sat next to Hugh and me were fascinating. He had never had soda before. When they placed the sugary, carbonated beverage in front of him, he looked very confused and continued to eat the goat and rice on his plate. After difficulty in trying to tell him what it was, he reluctantly took a sip. His eyes got really big and then the next thing we knew, he was chugging the entire thing. He didn't take a single bite after that. The disappointing thing about that is that at the restaurant, he had the opportunity to have his fill of so many nourishing, good-for-you foods that normally he wouldn't be able to have. Sure, the drink tasted delicious, but it wasn't going to ultimately fill him up with good things.

This resonates with me when I think of all the ways I try to satisfy my thirsty soul with the things of this world.

There are so many temporal pleasures in front of most of us that give us little sips of happiness and comfort. There have been seasons of my life where the distractions of the world seemed to be magnified, and, unfortunately, my lenses of God were blurred. We live in a society where we don't have to look farther than a screen in our hands to find something to ease boredom or discomfort.

Yet, in seasons of weakness?
In times where crisis hits and suffering abounds?
Suddenly, these things don't quite cut it.
We see them for what they are: temporary fixes.
Trinkets, not treasures.

And, in God's grace, we oftentimes are able to see
Him for who He is: the Fountain of Living Water.
The One who truly quenches our thirst with His limit-
less love, grace, and presence.
This, my friends, is what I think Paul means when he
talks about our weaknesses.

Scripture and our own life experiences show us that when we are stripped of everything we thought would fulfill us, the eyes of our heart are most likely to see the One who fulfills our every need in Himself. It is one thing for the watching world to see us walk through trials while grabbing for Band-Aids and gumballs to help us along the way. It's another thing altogether for the people around us to see our jars of clay, with nothing tangibly appeasing us, yet our hearts still encouraged in the midst of whatever circumstance we may be in. Only a Holy God is able to make us whole in the midst of our broken-ness. Only a Loving God has patience with us as we fumble around looking for sips of soda to get us by yet thirsty for more. Only a Mighty God can use our weakness to show His all-consuming strength and power even in the middle of our frail humanity.

That's the God I serve.

Today, it is the end of February 2018. While the month has not been as crisis-filled as this time last year, we certainly have had our share of unpredictable days. Seizures have showed up when least expected and made me shake in my own skin, yet God is showing me that it's okay to admit that my limitations give way to fear and anxiety, so long as I bring those to Him and leave them there.

"Cast your burden on the Lord, and He will sustain
you."

(Ps. 55:22a)

He will sustain you.

He will sustain you when it seems as if everything around you is falling apart. He will sustain you when you wake up in the middle of the night, and panic has overcome your body, and you feel as if you cannot breathe. He will sustain you when the cancer comes back or the wreck happens or the relationship ends or the friendship is betrayed or you're out of a job or even your own sin puts you in a position where it seems things will never get better. He will sustain.

His strength is strong in our weakness.
Your weakness does not scare Him—in fact, if He tells
us that He is strong in our weakness, then surely He's
not displeased with me when I am weak.
He knows you through and through, and He can
handle whatever this moment holds.

"Let anyone who is thirsty come to me and drink."

(John 7:37)

Today, may you drink in deeply the riches of our
unshakeable God.

30

MIDNIGHT

"About midnight Paul and Silas were praying and singing hymns to God, and the prisoners were listening to them."

(Acts 16:25)

Midnight is a hard hour to wake up around here. I don't know what it is about that time of night that seems so eerie.

Maybe it's that it is close enough to evening but far enough from dawn that it feels like the night is going to be long. It is smack-dab in the middle of the night, and for whatever reason, the dark feels even darker. A few nights ago, I woke up to the sound of gagging. This is oddly normal around here, so I jumped up out of bed and ran to the girls' room, only to find that I had not made it in time. The anonymous victim was now asleep (probably vomited in the middle of a seizure), yet covered in throw-up. I navigated getting sheets off and getting her into the bath (simply unavoidable at this point), which woke her up and, understandably, terrified her (I wouldn't want to wake up to the sound of water and a bright bathroom light, either). After getting her dressed and calmed down and back in bed, I went to the laundry room and cleaned the sheets off before checking the time.

Much to my disappointment, it was midnight.

I laid back down and tried to turn my brain off, falling back to sleep a little while later. The next wake-up proved to be shorter than the first, and I was relieved to look at my phone and see that it was 4:30 AM—what I consider almost morning.

> "...Weeping may tarry for the night, but joy comes with the morning."

> (Ps. 30:5)

With as many of God's truths that are still mysterious to me, this one makes absolute sense. I love the morning time, and I am very much a morning person. I tend to jump out of bed regardless of what our night held, and I treasure the moments where much of the world still sleeps, and I get to sit and spend time with the Lord in quiet. It does seem like no matter what happened during the night, the morning brings new mercies and the chance to start again.

In ways, I feel like this season of life is its own version of "midnight." We are in this continued season of waiting with the adoption, and the night seems long. Beyond that, as the girls get bigger and older, new challenges present themselves, and at times, I find myself more and more exhausted at the end of the day. I want to be a Proverbs 31 woman, a woman who "laughs at the time to come" (Prov. 31:25) not because it's going to be funny or even easy but because I simply trust the Lord; yet many days I find myself pushing through the trenches just waiting for my faith to have eyes.

> "So we do not lose heart. Though our outer self is wasting away, our inner self is being renewed day by day."

> (2 Cor. 4:16)

Not only were Paul and Silas in prison when they were praising God but also it was midnight. They were in that in-between place where they could have focused on how long the night might be; yet, they were fixated with the One who held all the stars in His hands.

> "...even the darkness is not dark to you; the night is
> bright as the day, for darkness is as light with you."

> (Ps. 139:12)

I honestly cannot think of anything more encouraging than the truth above. The very real reality is that with God, even the middle of the night feels like the dawn of day. He sees all. He knows all. He is above all. His light shines on everything and everyone at all times in all ways. I think Paul and Silas were able to sing in the night because they were beginning, by the grace of God, to grasp this. They saw their situation—the persecution, the pain, the less-than-ideal circumstance—and they rejoiced in it because they knew that no darkness they were walking through could escape the light of the Almighty.

> The dark seems really dark until it is contrasted with
> the Light.
> Midnight seems long unless we are focused on the
> One who is not limited by time.

A couple of years ago, Ally had a really bad case of bronchitis. We ended up going to Children's around 2:00 AM, but about midnight, I walked her out to the screened porch to see if the cooler air might help. As I held her in my arms, I felt the Lord nudge me out to the backyard. I instinctively looked up at the sky. It was a particularly star-filled night, and in my heart, I was reminded of these words:

"Lift up your eyes on high and see: who created these? He who brings out their host by number, calling them all by name, by the greatness of His might, and because He is strong in power not one is missing."

(Isa. 40:26)

In addition, a few verses down, this simple truth: "He does not faint or grow weary" (Isa. 40:28)

In those moments, my soul went into utmost praise. I did not know how long the night was going to be, yet I knew the One who held it all in the palm of His hand, and because of that, the rest faded into the background. Friend, God never grows weary in the night, no matter how long our night may seem. Beyond that, He is able to shine light into all the dark places of our lives and even our hearts.

After all, the dark is as light to Him.
In fact, it's why He came.

"The Spirit of the Lord God is upon me, because the Lord has anointed me to bring good news to the poor, He has sent me to bind up the brokenhearted, to proclaim liberty to the captives, and the opening of the prison to those who are bound; to proclaim the year of the Lord's favor, and the day of vengeance of our God; to comfort all who mourn; to grant to those who mourn in Zion- to give them a beautiful headdress instead of ashes, the oil of gladness instead of mourning, the garment of praise instead of a faint spirit; that they may be called oaks of righteousness, the planting of the Lord, that He may be glorified."

(Isa. 61:1–3)

One day, there will be a city that "has no need of sun or moon to shine on it," for "the glory of the Lord" will give it light, and "its lamp will be the Lamb" (Rev. 21:23).

I don't know where you find yourself today, but if it feels like midnight, I'm praying that the Lord would help you to remember His song in the night (Ps. 77:6). Because of Him, we have hope. Because of Him, we have light. Because of Him, we can praise Him in the midst of all. Just because you feel far from morning doesn't mean it's not coming. Look at the stars and remember, beloved.

> "For God who said, 'Let light shine out of darkness' has shone in our hearts to give the light of the knowledge of the glory of God in the face of Jesus Christ."

> (2 Cor. 4:6)

31

A FRAGRANT OFFERING

"And while He was at Bethany in the house of Simon the leper, as He was reclining at the table, a woman came with an alabaster flask of ointment of pure nard, very costly, and she broke the flask and poured it over His head. There were some who said to themselves indignantly, 'Why was the ointment wasted like that? For this ointment could have been sold for more than three hundred denarii and given to the poor.' And they scolded her. But Jesus said, "Leave her alone. Why do you trouble her? She has done a beautiful thing to me. For you always have the poor with you, and whenever you want, you can do good for them. But you will not always have me. She has done what she could..."'

(Mark 14:3–8a)

A few days ago, a roller full of the most expensive essential oil I own rolled off the shelf and down to the ground. It shattered everywhere; glass and oil all over the bathroom floor. It didn't take long for the rose oil to permeate the entire room, which would have been lovely except for the fact that it was all that I had.

"One of the Pharisees asked Him to eat with Him, and He went into the Pharisee's house and reclined at the table. And behold, a woman of the city, who was a sinner, when she learned He was reclining at the table in the Pharisee's house, brought an alabaster flask of ointment, and standing behind Him at His feet, weeping, she began to wet His feet with her tears and wiped them with the hair of her head and kissed His feet and anointed Him with an ointment. Now when the Pharisee who had invited Him saw this, he said to himself, 'If this man were a prophet, he would have known who and what sort of woman this is who is touching him, for she is a sinner.'"

(Luke 7:36–39)

Two separate scenes in Scripture, so many similarities. When you look at Jesus (which is who we want to focus on in every story!), you see a common theme of His showing up. Mark 14:3 says that Jesus was in the house of a leper. Luke 7:36 tells us that Jesus was visiting with a Pharisee. In both situations, it actually uses the same phrase: reclining at the table. To recline at the table didn't just mean he dropped a casserole off at the doorstep. To recline meant He was present, relaxed, and planning to stay for a while. A leper and a Pharisee might seem to have nothing in common, but the reality is that they had everything in common: they needed Jesus to make them clean from the inside out.

"…those who are well have no need of a physician, but those who are sick."

(Mark 2:17a)

When Jesus said these words, He was, in fact, reclining with tax collectors and sinners—a perfect storm for the Pharisees to show up. I love it that Jesus intentionally created environments in which He knew that a unique crowd would be drawn in. The "irony" doesn't escape me that Jesus saw it fit to bring unity among people that wouldn't normally step foot into the same markets, much less sit down at the same dinner table.

It's funny how God interrupts "our" plans, our thoughts, our ways in order to reiterate to us that His are different. A part of me wanted to push through and finish this chapter. Yet, God is doing something big and totally unexpected, and I'm not sure I can write a book about the intentionality and importance of every thread of our stories without demonstrating the pause button He pushes in each of our lives in order to show that He is living and active and working in all things. If you are like me, stopping in the middle is uncomfortable. I get frustrated when a television show or a movie leaves things open-ended. I don't even like it when I stop the gas pump on an odd number. Yet God. He calls us to the in-between and asks us to rest in Him right here, right now. So, together, let's leave this chapter open and move forward to what God is doing; these words are intentionally left for you to ponder on.

32

UNTRACEABLE

*"Oh, the depths of the riches and wisdom and knowledge
of God! How unsearchable are His judgments and how
inscrutable His ways!"*

(Rom. 11:33)

His paths beyond tracing out.
His decisions and His ways impossible to understand.
His judgments unfathomable.
His ways past finding out—untraceable, even.
These are some of the ways that various translations
word this verse.

I remember very little about kindergarten, yet I do recall getting back report cards. Back in the day that technology was minimal, you would get a piece of paper that graded different aspects of your learning abilities. Prior to first grade, you weren't judged with the A–F system but with E, S, NI, US (Excellent, Satisfactory, Needs Improvement, Unsatisfactory). Now, being a mom of twins with special needs has molded me to be less of a perfectionist, but back then I was quite the type-A little student. This meant that not only did I not really enjoy getting an *S* but also I actually preferred all *E*s. One day, as Mom pulled out my folder and saw the report, I could see the dismay in her eyes. *More S s than E s?* I thought. Knowing my own self-degrading tendencies, she gave a small smile and said, "Great job!" And then she mumbled, "And we can work on that."

Work on something?
I looked at the paper, and there it was:
An NI under tracing.
Sure there were several *E*s, but an NI?

From that moment forward, I made it my goal to practice tracing at every chance I got. I would ask my mom to draw lines and then I would use every writing utensil I could find to trace over said lines. I even asked my teacher to send home some practice sets. If improvement was needed, improvement was certainly going to happen.

"For my thoughts are not your thoughts, neither are your ways my ways, declares the Lord."

(Isa. 55:8)

We got our ninth no this morning, and I could not be more excited.
Let me explain.
The word inscrutable means "impossible to understand."
What I am about to tell you makes absolutely no sense to me from my very limited lens, yet I believe God has known about it from the beginning of time.
About two weeks ago, I was scrolling through my newsfeed and saw that an acquaintance had posted a picture of a six-year-old little boy from China. Also, this woman happened to be a former client from when I worked at the adoption agency. She has six children—three who were born in China—so she often advocates for orphans.

Normally, I would read—maybe pray—and probably move forward, yet this time my heart was stirred. I decided I would share the post about this little guy and offered some of my own personal thoughts on why someone should prayerfully ask the Lord whether or not that little boy could be theirs.

Little did I know that someone was going to be us.
I showed Hugh the picture, and about an hour later,
he posed a simple question:
"Hey, tell me more about that kid from China."

Now, you have to remember that over two years ago, Hugh and I both felt very much called to be in the domestic adoption process. We stepped forward in faith, and anytime we wondered whether or not we were hearing from God correctly, we continued to feel that this was the direction He was calling us. Flash-forward to these moments where neither Hugh nor I could get this little guy off our minds.

Have you ever asked the Lord to give you a sign only
to find that He gives you several?

"Then Gideon said to God, 'If you will save Israel by my hand, as you have said, behold, I am laying a fleece of wool on the threshing floor. If there is dew on the fleece alone, and it is dry on all the ground, then I shall know that you will save Israel by my hand, as you have said.' And it as so. When he rose early next morning and squeezed the fleece, he wrung enough dew from the fleece to fill a bowl with water. Then Gideon said to God, 'Let not your anger burn against me; let me speak just once more. Please let me test just once more with the fleece. Please let it be dry on the fleece only, and on all the ground let there be dew.' And God did so that night; and it was dry on the fleece only, and on all the ground there was dew."

(Judges 6:36–40)

What I am about to tell you felt as bizarre as it sounds. Sometimes, I can sense the Lord directly telling me something concerning details of my own life, yet, often, He simply requires steps of faith. He has told us all we need to know in His Word. The boundaries set and knowledge given are His to know and no one else's. Many times, I think we want God to give us clarity for a particular step He wants to take, yet, often, as Mother Teresa once said, "Clarity is the last thing we are clinging to and must let go of." Ultimately, God wants us to trust Him with all the details of our lives, whether we have had a big "aha" moment or not. Every now and then, however, I think He knows He's going to have to make something blatantly clear for ye—or *me*— of little faith to follow through. The story I'm sharing now qualifies as one of those times.

Hugh and I had been praying for a sign from the Lord that we were to step forward in pursuing this child from China instead of continuing in the domestic program. Last Tuesday, I sensed an inaudible nudge to open a book Hugh had just received from a friend to page 83. Now, mind you, 83 is not a significant number in my life. I hadn't been thinking about or looking at this book. At first, I ignored this, yet I could not get it off my mind, so I decided to just flip and see. An interesting fact is that this book is actually on orphans and the call of a Christian. As I turned to the page, I could not believe what I saw. It was the beginning of a chapter on orphans and poverty. Specifically, it was written by a man who had adopted a little boy from China, whose name was the exact name we had already predetermined we wanted to name a son. I took a picture of the page and sent it to Hugh.

I want to be careful in sharing too much or too little, yet trust me when I say that was the first of many nudges we have received in the last couple of weeks. Last week, we prayerfully said yes to showing our profile to a birth mom in the domestic adoption world. Now, normally, Hugh and I cannot wait to find out if we are chosen. We pray and we wait and we pray and we wait some more. This time, both of us began to hope that she would, in fact, say no to us. After receiving nine nos in the past two years, the longing to have another could be nothing but a sign from the Lord that He was planning "far more abundantly than all we ask or think" (Eph. 3:20).

We decided that we didn't want to withdraw from the process, however. We wanted this to be the final sign—our fleece, if you will. If God said no to this precious baby, we both knew what we felt like we were called to do next.

> "Trust in the Lord with all your heart, and do not lean on your own understanding. In all your ways acknowledge Him, and He will make straight your paths."
>
> (Prov. 3:5–6)

I have long prayed for a baby boy. It's a desire that seems to have been stirred in my heart for years now. There is absolutely no part of me— not a sliver—that ever intended to travel to China to bring home a child who is almost seven.

Yet God.

His love for us is so fierce—his love for this little boy is so fierce—that He would cause a friend from my small southern hometown to share a post about an orphan from a big city in China and press in on mine and Hugh's hearts so much so that we very much feel we couldn't say no even if we wanted to. A little boy who has been waiting for his entire life to be told, "Yes. Yes, we want you." A little boy who has completely replaced my desire for a teeny tiny little baby from the state of Alabama because now I realize that part of my heart evidently speaks Mandarin.

This is the love of the God we serve.
This is the path of the God we worship.
Untraceable, yet beautiful.
Beyond figuring out, yet glorious all the same.
"This God, His way is perfect." (Ps. 18:30)

As I'm typing this chapter, we have already received an e-mail letting us know the first few things we need to do to proceed.

I have absolutely no idea what this process is going to look like.
I don't know what obstacles are going to present themselves or what faith muscles are going to be stretched.
Yet, what I do know gives me peace for the things that are yet to be understood.

With God, it's okay if my tracing skills need improvement—I'm not meant to trace His ways; I'm made to trust His heart.

33

WE SAID YES

"For all the promises of God find their Yes in Him. That is why it is through Him that we utter our Amen to God for His glory."

(2 Cor. 1:20)

We said yes.

We sent off our Letter of Intent, and we waited. Less than six days later, we got the piece of paper that meant everything: we have been preapproved to adopt the little boy who we feel confident is our son.

You see the verse above? Yes is capitalized. In this case, Yes is a Person, and that Person is Jesus Christ. He is the forever Yes to all things good and true and lovely. He looks to humanity and says, "Yes. Yes, I took on your sin and shame. Yes, I conquered death. Yes, I am coming back."

Ten nos.

If I'm honest, I don't remember the specific details of each of them, but there are certainly a handful that stand out. I remember the first. We will call her Breanna. In the days that we waited, I went to cash a check at the bank, and when I got the receipt, she signed it with her name: Breanna.

I was sure that was a sign.

After getting the e-mail that said we were, in fact, not chosen, I was confused yet confident our day would quickly come.

On a cold, atypically snowy day in Alabama this January, it had been two years and nine nos, and I remember sitting as I watched the sun come up and wondering what in the world God was doing.

Had He forgotten us?
Had He put us in this position for the very intention
of hurting us?

I knew these things not to be true, yet my heart burned, and in ways, the crispy edges of a hope that seemed to be deferred were starting to boil up.

A few weeks later at church, we were in the midst of a sermon series on Nehemiah. The focus verse on the front of the bulletin read this:

> "I told them how the gracious hand of my God had been on me, and what the king had said to me. They said, 'Let's start rebuilding,' and their hands were strengthened to do this good work."
>
> (Neh. 2:18)

As we stood up and worshipped together, I heard that familiar, most-comforting inaudible voice whisper, "Something is coming, and it is of the Lord."

I sat down and wrote that right beside the verse on the front cover.

A part of me wondered if I had made it all up. Our hearts are deceptive, and, oh, how vastly different yet fine the line is between the Spirit and our emotions.

Yet, as His plans began to unfold in the coming weeks, I knew that this new assignment was exactly what He had been assuring me a few Sundays before.

The day we got the e-mail for pre-approval, I read back over this verse: "Their hands were strengthened to do this good work," the last part of it read.

And isn't that why we are given the privilege to say yes to anything put in front of us by God Himself?

> 2 Corinthians 1:20 proclaims it loud and clear:
> It is only through Him we can confidently utter our
> Amen to whatever His paths unfold.

> "For the promise to Abraham and his offspring that he
> would be heir of the world did not come through the
> law but through the righteousness of faith...the words
> "it was counted to him" were not written for his sake
> alone, but for ours also. It will be counted to us who
> believe in him who raised from the dead Jesus Christ
> our Lord, who was delivered up for our trespasses and
> raised for our justification."

> (Rom. 4:13, 23–25)

> We are saved by grace through faith alone.

> All our righteous deeds are like a polluted garment in
> light of the perfection of God

> (Isa. 64:6).

The weakness of God is stronger than any man's strength

(1 Cor. 1:25).

And so, moving forward, we aren't saying yes to an agency or to China or really even to this child in particular. We are saying yes to God Himself—the Ultimate Yes—who gives us the ability to say yes to all the things in the first place!

We love because He first loved us

(1 John 4:19).

There will be a lot that we don't know until we actually have our son with us. While we might be blessed to have files and pictures and videos, ultimately the plan will unfold once he is officially home with us.

We don't know a lot, but here's what we do know: we know that God is for us. We know that God has known this child—His child— since the beginning and that all the days of his life have been written before, yet one of them came to be (Ps. 139:16). We know that God goes before and behind and that He knows exactly what we are do-ing. We know that He is going to equip us in this journey as we go along. We know that His ways are perfect (Deut. 32:4). We know He is a good, good Father. The truth is, in the midst of all of our stories, what we do not know is microscopic compared to all that we do know through Christ Jesus. It's not what we know but Who we know that changes everything. And, ultimately, we are well-acquainted with the One who is more acquainted with us than we are with ourselves, the One who is sovereignly working out all things for His glory and our good.

We say yes to uncertain, often hard things not to prove our love for Him but because we have experienced and believed His love for us.

In the midst of all those nos, I had so many questions. I still am working through what in the world God was doing during the season Hugh and I were sitting in the domestic adoption program assuming we were going to be receiving a yes from a birth mom pregnant with a tiny infant, knowing perfectly well we had a six-year-old son in China. I don't think I will receive that answer on this side of heaven, yet by the grace of God this I know with a humble confidence:

The love of Christ always surpasses worldly knowledge

(Eph. 3:19).

God is an active God, and He is always working in our waiting.

"But now, O Lord, You are our Father; we are the clay, and You are our potter; we are all the work of Your hand."

(Isa. 64:8)

God has been up to something so much greater than we could comprehend, abundantly more even, these past couple of years.

So it is with your life.

I don't know what chapter you are living out today; I'm not sure why God has you in what might feel like a standstill or, even sometimes worse, in the midst of His deafening silence. Yet, here's what I want you to do. I want you to pick up a Bible and turn to Hebrews 11. I want you to read through the entire chapter and then I want you to get to verses 39—40 and read it aloud:

"And all these, though commended through their
faith, did not receive what was promised, since God
had provided something better for us, that apart from
us they should not be made perfect."

Apart from us—apart from you and your individually handpicked story—God's gloriously eternal story is not finished. This chapter of your life—with all its details—matters. And the God who calls you wants to equip you, strengthen you, help you to receive limitlessly more of Him in the midst.

The God who cried "It is finished," isn't finished with
you yet.
We love because He first loved us.

May all that we say and all that we do and all that we are be a living, moving, breathing representation of this—and all our yeses be made yes in Him. He is the One. The One who said yes to us when He breathed life into us, who said yes to us as He hung on the cross on our behalf, who says, "Yes, I will be with you in the midst of whatever high or low you are walking through," the One who, on that glorious day, will say yes to us as we enter into His presence and His kingdom forever.

Come, Lord Jesus.
Amen.

34

FOR THE ONE

*"... What man of you, having a hundred sheep, if he has
lost one of them, does not leave the ninety-nine in the open
country, and go after the one that is lost, until he finds
it? And when he has found it, he lays it on his shoulders,
rejoicing. And when he comes home, he calls together his
friends and his neighbors, saying to them, 'Rejoice with me, for
I have found my sheep that was lost.' Just so, I tell you, there
will be more joy in heaven over one sinner who repents than
over ninety-nine righteous persons who need no repentance."*

(Luke 15:3–7)

I can't think about traveling to China past about 8:30 PM. There is something about being tired that magnifies emotions and blurs truth, and by about 9:00 PM, this early riser is tired and needs to turn off her thinking brain. In a few months, Hugh and I will travel to bring our son home. It will be a 10- to 14-day trip, and while this may not sound like long to many of you, we have not left our girls for more than two nights since they were born. There are so many uncertainties about our girls' health on any given day, and the longer the travel, the more likely something will come up. As we were praying through whether or not we felt like this, in fact, was the child God wanted to entrust to our family next, one of my biggest barriers (also known as one of the things I was having a hard time trusting God with) was this whole idea of leaving the girls for so long. We mentioned it to our nurses before even telling our family, and all three of them gave a resounding "Of course, we will be able to help in whatever way we are needed." The reality is, God has graced us with much more support than most people in our situation. It's not that we don't have great options for help with our girls while we are gone; it's simply that there are so many unknowns involved in leaving them for an extended period of time.

> "And He said to all, 'If anyone would come after me, let him deny himself and take up his cross daily and follow me. For whoever would save his life will lose it but whoever loses his life for my sake will save it.'"

(Luke 9:23–24)

Oftentimes, losing our life comes in the form of laying down seemingly small idols over and over. It's choosing God when choosing self or control might be easier. It's letting go of comfort and ease and picking up the hard thing in light of the fact that He goes with you. It's wanting to do x but deciding to do y because you would rather "be a doorkeeper in the house of your God than dwell in the tents of the wicked" (Ps. 84:10).

The reality is, some martyrs die at the stake but most simply yet profoundly continue to keep their eyes on Jesus at the cross—and, alas, at the right hand of God! — repeatedly.

Cory Asbury's song "Reckless Love" (2017) has been the theme of our house in the midst of this adoption. As I was listening to our girls babble on and on through one of the verses, this line pierced my heart in a new way:

"Oh, the overwhelming, never-ending, reckless love of God. Oh, it chases me down, fights til I'm found, leaves the ninety-nine. I couldn't earn it, I don't deserve it, still You give Yourself away."

While we were yet sinners, Christ died for us.

(Rom. 5:8)

Two verses before are these glorious words:

While we were still weak, at the right time Christ died for the ungodly

(Rom. 5:6).

I cannot comprehend this love. I have never nor ever will be loved again in this way, yet I don't need to be, for His love endures forever.

I believe with all my heart that either Ally or Bailey Grace will be given the ability to understand the Gospel or they will simply be treated like a child from their first breath until their last when they meet Him face-to-face. I cannot reconcile some of the theological processes that go along with this reality, yet I believe it to be true. They are our children, entrusted to Hugh and me for however long of a season the Lord sees fit. They hear the Gospel in some form each and every day.

In these very moments, there is a six-year-old boy in China who I feel fairly confident has never heard of Jesus. He hasn't heard the promises of a God who will ultimately never leave us as orphans. He does not know the glorious reality of a God who gives us a "reckless love" that we could never earn or deserve. Jesus is Immanuel, God with us. In Christ, we are reconciled to a holy God and now, in right relationship with Him forever, not based on anything we have done or ever could do but relying on His glorious grace. God will never leave us, yet Luke 15 tells us the importance of each and every one of His children by telling us that all the saints rejoice whenever one sheep is reunited with His Shepherd—so much so that it's worth leaving the 99 who have already been found.

God's Word makes it clear in both the parable of the lost sheep and the parable of the lost coin and of the prodigal son: every single soul is precious and valuable to Him, and He goes to great lengths to show us His abounding love for us.

In light of that, how could we *not* leave our 99 and go to China to bring home the one?

I have come to see that some of the greatest blessings in our life have come from the greatest risks.

If you would have told me all that we would have gone through with Ally and Bailey Grace, I can humbly admit I am not sure I would have been brave enough to have chosen this story. Knowing them now, however, I would never choose another one. No matter how hard or easy pieces of our lives are, they are just that; ours, given by a gracious God who is writing each and every detail. God is meticulous in all His ways. So many times we are waiting for a certain season to pass when I think God is saying, "I'm here! I'm here! I want you to see me here."

As we wait to bring our son home, I can quickly jump to the "there." It's easy for me to think that "there" will bring more assurance, more comfort, more satisfaction even. But God. He always reminds us that it's here in these very crevices that He is working and molding and doing the things far beyond what we can comprehend.

I don't know what our time in China will look like. Moving forward, I'm not sure all the hards that will be included in this part of the story. But I know He's good, and that's what keeps me pressing forward. I know our little boy has been ours from the moment His Creator intricately made him in his birth mother's womb. I know that regardless of when or what or how, God is in China. God is in Alabama. He will be in China, and He will be in Alabama from the moment our plane lands until the day when we bring our son home. I also know that He is wherever you are too, and I don't just mean literally. Whatever season you are in, the same God who always chooses to leave the 99 for the one, He's calling out to you too. And if that's you—if you are the sheep who turned to the right or the left because it seemed like there was something better and suddenly you find yourself broken and confused and lost—He's with you.

"Let the little children come to me and do not hinder them, for to such belongs the kingdom of heaven."

(Matt. 19:14)

To such belongs the kingdom of heaven.
Like a child, might you rest in His presence today.
Don't worry about what's ahead; He's got that all planned.
Simply rest in the love of the Shepherd, the Good Shepherd, who knows His sheep and is always longing to bring you back into the fold.
Oh, taste and see that the Lord is good.

35

GOD IS FOR ME

There is something so cathartic about writing while the girls are still sleeping. It's 7:30 in the morning; normally, we would be rushing to get ready for the school day. The past few weeks have included asthmatic coughing for Ally and lots of seizing and vomiting for Bailey Grace, so when they both were still asleep when it was time to get up for the day, I decided to simply let them sleep until their bodies decided it was time to wake up. Somehow, I feel like I'm able to focus more whenever they are peaceful in their beds. Even when they are away from me, lately my mind can become consumed with how they are doing. Is Bailey Grace seizing yet? Is she having an easy or hard morning? Has she been engaged and able to participate or absent and in her own world? Is Ally coughing a lot? Does she seem like she's ready to be back to school or needed another day at home? Did I give her enough breathing treatments, or does her chest feel tight? These thoughts can reign in my mind even as I attempt to do all the things. My heart knows truth, that God is there with them, that He loves them more than I ever could, that He knows what He is doing. But these circumstances. They can get heavy and daunting, even when I'm simply to carry them to the cross.

But is the cross where I'm supposed to leave them,
anyway?

If we really think about it, maybe the point is not to leave our burdens at the cross but to trust they are already overcome by the One on the throne. After all, *He* carried them on our behalf.

Maybe they simply aren't mine to mess with at all.

"Be gracious to me, O God, for man tramples on me; all day long an attacker oppresses me; my enemies trample on me all day long."

(Ps. 56:1–2)

All day long.

Do you ever feel like that? Do you ever feel like you have an Enemy that is literally spending every waking (or even sleeping) hour throwing darts at you?

There's a song that Sovereign Grace Music sings, "O Lord, My Rock and My Redeemer" (2017), written by Nathan Stiff, and one of the verses says this:

O Lord, my Rock and my Redeemer
Strong defender of my weary heart
My sword to fight the cruel deceiver
And my shield against his hateful darts
My song when enemies surround me
My hope when tides of sorrows rise
My joy when trials are abounding
Your faithfulness, my refuge in the night

It seems these words are much easier for me to sing when I'm in the midst of community, daylight shining through the windows of the sanctuary, and when it's one in the morning and one child is coughing up blood and the other is seizing and the darts are actually being shot our way.

The past few weeks have been back to hard. I say back because, while these years with Ally and Bailey Grace have never been a breeze, we have had a refreshing season of minimal crisis and rest. For a few months now, new seizure mystery has appeared for Bailey Grace, and it's been days of unpredictability and at times simply trying to survive. Do you ever have seasons where you are painfully aware at how hateful Satan's darts absolutely are? It's weird. We can go from being tempted to sin (our flesh) to realizing how evil and futile and gross sin is (the Spirit), all in a few minutes. So goes our humanity.

> "All day long they injure my cause; all their thoughts against me for evil. They stir up strife, they lurk; they watch my steps, as they have waited for my life...You have kept count of my tossings; put my tears in Your bottle. Are they not in Your book? Then my enemies will turn back in the day when I call. This I know, that God is for me. In God, whose word I praise, in the Lord, whose word I praise, in God I trust; I shall not be afraid...for You have delivered my soul from death, yes, my feet from falling, that I may walk before God in the light of life."

> (Ps. 56:5–6, 8–11, 13)

Two nights ago, we woke up to a painfully familiar cry. When Ally has a cough, she will often wake up in the middle of the night and feel as if she cannot breathe. I can't imagine how terrifying that is for her; not only is that jarring to wake up to but also she has the obstacle of figuring out how to get her parents up there as quickly as possible so that she doesn't choke as she begins to cough. I always pray the girls know they are never alone—even when we cannot physically be there. I am comforted to know that God says He puts our tears in a bottle. Not only does He put them in any bottle; He collects them in His very bottle. This lets me know both that He intimately cares about our every hurt and that He takes responsibility for bringing good from them. After all, God doesn't waste anything, and why gather tears you aren't going to use? When my momma heart hurts for my children—for Ally and Bailey Grace who have so many sufferings that even though I desperately want to walk with them, I simply can't fully understand—for our son who has had six years in China and now sits in an orphanage, waiting for us to come, I remind myself of these truths. God is there. He cares more than I ever could. And—and this one is key—He is for us.

> This I know, that God is for me
>
> (Ps. 56:9b).

> We ask each other the question all the time: "How are you?"
> We throw it out flippantly to one another, "Hope you're having a good day!"

But when chronic suffering hits, these questions can feel like salt to a wound. The truth is, I don't know how to answer those formalities when Bailey Grace has been seizing on and off all day, and there are towels covered in vomit that I don't have time to clean because I'm holding her as her brain continues to misfire. I'm not sure what the appropriate response is when we've been up most of the night tending to Ally who screams and coughs up blood, giving us a terrified look that says to me, "When are you going to make this stop? Please make it stop."

How am I?
Am I having a good day?
These old tapes play like a horror movie even on the
less traumatic days, and no longer does cultural lingo
seem to apply.
This I know: that God is for me.
This I know: that God is for me.
This I know: that God is for me.

What if we had recordings of His truths playing so loudly in our heads and our hearts that the fleeting reality of our circumstances suddenly felt like a whisper?

What if we stopped counting good days and started calling all days God days?

Friend, I have to believe that every single tear I cry, every single tear my children cry, goes into the possession of the God of the universe who wastes absolutely nothing. When my son was an infant—before I even knew he was—I have to trust that God was there and that even if no one else heard his cries, God did, and He was absolutely storing up those precious little tears for His glory and that beautiful little boy's good. When it's the middle of the night, and Hugh and I are fast asleep, and Bailey Grace's brain wakes her up for yet again another seizure—who knows how many for the night—I have to trust that He very much so does not slumber or sleep, and He is a very present help in her trouble. I have to make a choice to open God's Word and, if even through clenched teeth, shout the praises of the One who is in control and working out all things for His good even when I can't see an ounce of beauty in the midst of all the ashes.

What the Enemy intends for evil, God has always intended for good

(Gen. 50:20).

When Satan lurks, seeking to kill, steal, and destroy, and the darts feel like they are coming from every single direction, He hems me in, behind, and before

(Ps. 139:5).

The truth is, we can focus on all the places the difficulties are firing from, or we can fixate on the One who is an all-consuming fire

(Deut. 4:24).

The Enemy of your soul may be hell-bent on your destruction all the day long, but if in Christ, all of his efforts are futile.
Your soul has already been won by the blood of Jesus.
Your future is secure.
Your suffering has an expiration date.

His position is firm at the right hand of the Father, pleaded on our behalf

(Heb. 7:25).

We may spend the rest of our days on earth in the battle, but one day, this will be our story:

"He will dwell with them, and they will be his people, and God himself will be with them as their God. He will wipe away every tear from their eyes, and death shall be more, neither shall there be mourning, nor crying, nor pain anymore, for the former things have passed away."

(Rev. 21:3b–4)

He is making all things new, and we will spend eternity praising Him all the day long.
This light and momentary trouble is producing in us something that can't compare.
His victory already happened.
Joy is imminent.
Jesus is here.
I don't have to know anything else if this I know: God is for me.

36

THE END OF THE MATTER

I don't know why it took me so long to realize I adore Hallmark movies. When I was really in the middle of the "warm and fuzzy, we call it the Christmas spirit, but really it might just be the spirit of twinkling lights and Frazier tree smells" mode, I grasped the knowledge that not only were there Christmas Hallmark movies but also year-round movies that aligned with whatever particular season we were in. This floored me, and in my mind I pictured myself basking in feel-good scripts for pretty much forever. I confess I have not watched a single movie since that last week of December, but I did briefly turn to a Valentine's Day one in which I realized pretty quickly the decorations were different but the scenario was about the same. It was glorious. Most days, if I'm watching the television, I would much rather watch something realistic. I love crime shows and, yes, on more than a few occasions, have been known to watch *Live PD* or *The First 48*. Some might say they are depressing, but to me they are such a depiction of humanity and our brokenness and God and His goodness. The weird part is, as far from accurate as those Hallmark movies might seem from 99.9 percent of our lives, I think we like them so much because there is a part of us that knows we were made for the happy ending.

"As for me, Daniel, my spirit within me was anxious, and the visions of my head alarmed me. I approached one of those who stood there and asked him the truth concerning all this. So he told me and made known to me the interpretation of the things. These four great beasts are four kinds who shall arise out of the earth. But the saints of the Most High shall receive the kingdom and possess the kingdom forever, forever and ever. Then I desired to know the truth about the fourth beast, which was different from all the rest, exceedingly terrifying, with its teeth of iron and claws of bronze, and which devoured and broke in pieces and stamped what was left with its feet, and about the ten horns that were on its head, and that had eyes and a mouth and spoke great things, and that seemed greater than its companions. As I looked, this horn made war with the saints and prevailed over them, until the Ancient of Days came, and judgment was given for the saints of the Most High, and the time came when the saints possessed the kingdom. Thus he said: 'As for the fourth beast, there shall be a fourth kingdom on earth, which shall be different from all the kingdoms, and it shall devour the whole earth, and trample it down, and break it to pieces. As for the ten horns, out of this kingdom ten kings shall arise, and another shall arise after them; he shall be different from the former ones, and shall put down three kings. He shall speak words against the Most High, and shall wear out the saints of the Most High, and shall think to change the times and the law; and they shall be given into his hand for a time, times, and half a time. But the court shall sit in judgment, and his dominion shall be taken away, to be consumed and destroyed to the end. And the kingdom and the dominion and the greatness of the kingdoms

under the whole heaven shall be given to the people
of the saints of the Most High; his kingdom shall be
an everlasting kingdom, and all dominions shall serve
and obey Him.' Here is the end of the matter."

(Dan. 7:15–28a)

Before we continue, let's note two things: number one, I am no Bible
scholar. I have loved and cherished and studied and meditated on
God's Word for as long as I can remember, yet my formal training
is not just minimal but zero. Number two is that I would also like
to note I might go down as the first person to write a chapter that
includes both deep theological truths from Daniel as well as the
Hallmark channel. I'm not sure if you should be proud or concerned,
but, either way, stick with me. The basic synopsis of what's going on
in the above readings is that Daniel has had a vision, and there is an
angel who is interpreting the said vision. There are four beasts in the
vision, and Daniel seems particularly distressed and confused by the
fourth. There is disagreement about who or what exactly the fourth
beast is, yet one thing is clear: though the beast will attempt to wear
out the saints of the Most High, the Ancient of Days ultimately has
the victory. Though this beast will try to destroy God's people, he will
eventually and assuredly be the one that is destroyed.

God always wins.
Here is the end of the matter.

I relate to Daniel here because, really, I just want to know that all this
is going to turn out not only for good but also for a purpose. When
I watch a Hallmark movie, during the ten minutes that the businesswoman has decided that she's going to go back to the big city and
be a businesswoman instead of a small-town girl after all, I'm not
stressing. Why? Because I know where the thing is headed. The track
record is clear: she's going to change her mind. She's going to make a

last-minute decision before the plane boards or before the big meeting with the CEO, and she's going to turn around and head back toward the place where she truly belongs. Hallmark has simply never failed me on this. Not once has the movie turned out for anything but mushy, glorious good.

> On an eternally greater, bigger scale, so goes God's kingdom.

> "God is light, in Him is no darkness at all."

> (1 John 1:5)

This is a truth we can hang our hat on. This is an anchor we can completely secure our souls on. This is a reality that there is not even a tiny portion—not a millisecond of a millisecond—where God is anything but Light and His plans are anything but perfect.

His track record shows nothing but perfection, in fact.

This week has felt really dark, not only in the world but also in our little corner of it. Bailey Grace had a planned admission to the hospital where we attempted to get a grip on what these new episodes she has been having are, and the attempt was unsuccessful. She didn't have a single event while we were there, except for the first hour prior to us getting to a room. We had prayed fervently that He would give us wisdom and discernment from this visit; was He not listening?

> "How long O Lord? Will you forget me forever? How long will you hide your face from me? How long must I take counsel in my soul and have sorrow in my heart all the day? How long shall my enemy be exalted over me?"

> (Ps. 13:1–2)

I relate to the Psalmist here because there are times where I feel like God continually gives us the exact opposite of what we have asked Him for. Particularly for our precious Bailey Grace, this season is full of simply one thing after another. We didn't find answers to the questions we had about her current neurological episodes; instead, we found more questions and more issues to investigate. Why?

Sometimes, that's my simple yet profound question to Him: why? Why has the answer been no to so many of the prayers we have uttered to You?

"For I do not want you to be unaware, believers, that our fathers were all under the cloud (in which God's presence went before them) and they all passed (miraculously and safely) through the (Red) Sea, and all (of them) were baptized into Moses (into his safekeeping as their leader) in the cloud and in the sea, and all (of them) ate the same spiritual food; and all (of them) drank the same spiritual drink, for they were drinking from a spiritual rock which followed them; and the rock was Christ. Nevertheless, God was not well-pleased with most of them, for they were scattered along the ground in the wilderness (because their lack of self-control led to disobedience which led to death). Now these things (these warnings and admonitions) took place as examples for us, so that we would not crave evil things as they did. Do not be worshipers of handmade gods, as some of them were; just as it is written (in Scripture), 'The people sat down to eat and drink (after sacrificing to the golden calf at Horeb), and stood up to play (indulging in immoral activities).' We must not indulge in (nor tolerate) sexual immorality, as some of them did, and twenty-three thousand (suddenly) fell dead in a single day!

We must not tempt the Lord (that is, test His patience, question His purpose or exploit His goodness), as some of them did—and they were killed by serpents. And do not murmur (in unwarranted discontent), as some of them did- and they were destroyed by the destroyer. Now these things happened to them as an example and warning (to us); they were written for our instruction (to admonish and equip us), upon whom the ends of the ages have come."

(1 Cor. 10:1–11)

In the Garden, before Eve took a bite of the apple and God's great rescue of His children began to play out, God had given Adam and Eve immense freedom. God has always been about freeing, not enslaving. He desired for Adam and Eve to bask in and enjoy all the glorious things He had created. God's one request was for their good: do not eat the fruit from that one tree. You can eat anything else, yet just trust me when I say do not eat from that one.

God is God, and I am not, and that is a good, good
thing.

This was the basic premise for His reasons behind this one command. When Eve determined to take matters into her own hands (women, I think we are pretty good at this one), things took a turn, and suddenly Adam and Eve's relationship with both God and each other was changed.

God still had a plan.
He always has, you know.

The rest of the Bible—and the remainder of all time, really—plays out the details of God reconciling Himself to His children. The verses above in 1 Corinthians 10 flesh out a horrifically great depiction of the ways we try and take things into our own hands:

We look to other things or people to satisfy.
We question His goodness in what He is doing.
We complain about our circumstances.
Essentially, we turn from Thee and turn straight to "me."

It didn't ever turn out well for the Israelites, and it certainly never turns out well for us, either.

As I've wrestled with God over the current whys in this story, I'm realizing that, really, I don't want to know why. I simply want to know how long.

How long until He makes it all right? How long until
He shows Himself victorious?
The waiting can be painful.

"No temptation has overtaken you that is not common to man. God is faithful, and He will not let you be tempted beyond your ability, but with the temptation He will also provide the way of escape, that you may be able to endure it."

(1 Cor. 10:13)

I used to view these verses in light of whatever external sin I was currently struggling with. Be it drinking too much in college, sexual sin before marriage, or gossiping with my sorority sisters (how basic can I sound?), I thought these truths implied that when I felt tempted to do something wrong, God would always help me stay strong and do the right thing. In some ways, I still believe this to be true; however, now I interpret these verses differently. In light of where they land, this comes right after the above verses that talk about the Israelites and the ways they displeased the Lord. Beyond specific action, Paul notes the state of the people's hearts as the reason for God being displeased. Their obsession with figuring out what God was doing caused them to forget both all He had already done and all that He had promised to do.

Isn't this us?

When we ask God why: why He is allowing trials to come in waves; why He didn't heal our loved one when we prayed so confidently; why we seem to be the target for betrayal and insult; why we can't seem to get a break financially, relationally, physically, what we are really asking is why He isn't choosing to do things "our" way.

When Jesus was in the Garden of Gethsemane, the Bible makes it clear that He was beyond distressed. He was pleading and praying and asking the Lord to take the cup away, and then one short sentence said it all:

"Yet not my will but yours." (Luke 22:42)
Jesus—fully God, fully man.
Jesus—sinless within Himself.
Jesus— the Son of the God of the universe.

He was about to walk the road of Calvary, carrying a cross and dying a death that He absolutely did nothing to deserve. Yes, He asked for a way out. Yes, He pleaded with the Father momentarily. But then? Then He went forward confidently in the plans that had been laid out before the beginning of time. You see, He didn't ask why in these moments because in these moments, He knew that the Father was still with Him. The only time "why" was ever uttered from His mouth was as He hung from the cross, bleeding out for you and for me. In His dying breath, He sputtered,

"My God, my God, why have you forsaken me?"

(Matt. 27:46)

Because Jesus willingly chose the cross—because He uttered this unfathomable why—we both have absolutely no right and absolutely no reason to ask God "why" ever again.

Jesus made it all right.
Jesus sealed the already set truth that whatever God
was going to do moving forward was for our good and
His glory.

"He who did not spare His own Son but gave Him up for us all, how will He not also with Him graciously give us all things?"

(Rom. 8:32)

Oh, beloved, it is finished. We don't have to know why. He is working it all out for His glory and our good. He is for us. All His ways are good. We don't have to know what He's doing to know He's doing something.

So in the midst of this painful piece of the magnificent story that only He knows all the details to, I can cling to and trust Him and know He is with us. I can believe He loves my Bailey Grace more than I ever could—even when I cannot see it. And guess what? So can you in whatever chapter you are in. His track record is sure. He knows what He is doing. If in Christ, we will, one day, live happily ever after—no Hallmark set required.

This, my friends, is the end of the matter.

37

NOT THERE...YET

What is it that's so great about the weekend?

A s a kid, I remember so vividly the excitement of knowing that
Friday was coming. A lot of times, Friday nights were spent
with a friend at my house, watching TGIF and eating stuffed
crust Pizza Hut pizza. I don't really remember why slumber parties
were so fun, but I do recall counting down the hours until school was
over and the party began.

Speaking of parties, high school and college made the weekend
seem all the more glorious. At the time, to say my priorities were out
of whack would be an understatement. While I knew of the Lord during these years, it was the end of my adolescence and beginning of my
twenties that I believe I came to an understanding that knowledge of
the Lord versus knowing the Lord and desiring Him to be Lord over
your life were two very different things. That being said, weekends
during my time at UGA were often all about me: what I wanted to
do, with whomever I wanted to do it, whenever I chose. Still, it had a
familiar free feeling that Friday to Sunday always did.

My dad and I have always talked about that Sunday-night feeling.

It's hard to describe, but for years, it creeped up around the time
the sun was going to go down on a Sunday evening. Looking back, I
think I magnified the weekend so much so that it teetered on idolatry,

so it makes sense that I would get a funny feeling when the thing I had placed my affection on was beginning to fade away. During residency years, weekends didn't exist. Hugh rarely had a consecutive Saturday and Sunday off, so this whole idea of a weekend really lost its luster. It sounds funny, but I really believe God used that season to break me of self in a lot of ways, one of them being the expectations I had always placed on the end of the week.

These days, Hugh has most weekends off, and in ways they are certainly a reprieve of sorts. Our life with Ally and Bailey Grace has changed the way I view our time immensely, so while I don't have this huge expectation of escape and fun every time Saturday comes around, I do feel grateful for a couple of days to take a deep breath and relax a little more.

Unlike the Friday-night slumber parties of the nineties, though, time seems to be flying.

Before my dad's mom passed away, I remember talking to her about getting older. I will never forget a conversation we had about how she felt when she passed a mirror. She told me that many days, she would pass a mirror and think, *I wonder who that old lady is*, only to realize that it was herself. She talked to me about how fast time began to go by the more that it passed, and since I've been a parent, I could not agree more. When I was younger, it felt like I was able to experience the present more fully. Why? I'm not sure. Technology has certainly challenged all of our abilities to be in the moment, yet I think even before social media and Wi-Fi, our elders felt the same way.

But is life really going faster, or are we just paying less attention?

"Then Moses said to God, 'If I come to the people of Israel and say to them, "The God of your fathers has sent me to you," and they ask me, "What is his name?" what shall I say to them?' God said to Moses, 'I AM

WHO I AM.' And He said, 'Say this to the people of
Israel, "I AM has sent me to you."'"

(Exod. 3:13–14)

His name is I AM, not I was or I will be. Yet—

"I AM the Alpha and the Omega…who is and who was
and who is to come, the Almighty."

(Rev. 1:8)

The Almighty who has absolutely complete power.

The Almighty, the One who both causes grief, yet does
not afflict from His heart.

(Lam. 3:31, 33)

So goes our God. He is God with us in these moments—yes, even
these. He is in the between, yet goes before and behind. He never
once—no, not for a second—leaves or forsakes.

But today in the here and now, it can feel so dark and so lonely,
and there are days that it seems we are walking through a desert just
begging for one tiny sip of water to quench our weary souls.

Yet somehow, by the grace that keeps our very lungs breathing
and our very hearts beating, we are kept.

These days, they can be long. And, somehow, it seems in the
longest of days we are even more tempted to speed by the very things
that God is doing. We, like the Israelites, can look back and say—

"What have you done to us in bringing us out of Egypt?"

(Exod. 14:11)

We hear of His salvation and His rescue of us, we mostly believe it for what's to come, but today we are left wondering why we couldn't have just stayed in the slavery that may have been different than what we were created for but at least, in our humanity, felt comfortable.

So I will ask it again:
Is life really going faster, or are we just paying less attention?

Friend, I know. I know the longer we live, the more trials we experience, and so often it's tempting to just want to press fast-forward or even try to find another script because surely this isn't the one He intended.

But God.
He is the Almighty.
I Am who I say I Am.
His grace is a very present help, both on our best and worst days.
His plans for us do not change based on our fleeting emotions or the actions or decisions of those around us.
He knows exactly what He is doing, and He beckons us to be here, now.
There is a way to get caught up in the moment in the wrong way, yet—thanks be to God—there is a way to get swept up in the moment the right way.

The same God who says, "For everything there is a season, and a time for every matter under heaven," continues *that very same chapter* promising "He has made everything beautiful in its time" (Eccles. 3:1, 11a).

And also?

"He has put eternity into man's heart, yet so that he
cannot find out what God has done from the beginning to the end."

(Eccles. 3:11b)

Deep inside, we know.

Regardless of how many layers we have tried to add to cover it up, no
matter how many times we have attempted to push rewind or fast-
forward, here in this present moment we know that He created us for
something more.

"If I find in myself desires which nothing in this world
can satisfy, the only logical explanation is that I was
made for another world." (C. S. Lewis)
No, this isn't it. Yet, God in His wisdom has you here, now.

There is something intimately, intentionally, exquisitely important about
this very millisecond—with all its circumstantial twists and turns—the
most important one being that God is sovereignly here and actively working on something gloriously beyond that which we can comprehend.

One day, the fog will be lifted.

"For now we see in a mirror dimly, but then face to
face. Now I know in part; then I shall know fully, even
as I have been fully known."

(1 Cor. 13:12)

No, we are not there yet.
But by dross consumed and gold refined, Christian,
oh, we shall be.

REFERENCES

All Scripture, unless otherwise noted, are taken from the Holy Bible, English Standard Version.

Lewis, C. S. "Friendship." In *The Four Loves*. San Diego: Harcourt, Inc., 1960, 65.

Peterson, Eugene. "Preface." In *As Kingfishers Catch Fire*. New York: Waterbrook, 2017, xvii.

Foreword:
Keen, Robert. *How Firm a Foundation*, 1787.
Lewis, C. S. *Mere Christianity*. San Francisco, HarperOne, 2015.

Feeble Hands:
Bianco, Margery Williams. *The Velveteen Rabbit*. Kennebunkport, Maine: Appleseed Press Book Publishers, 2012, vol. 8, 10–11.

Misplaced Shame:
"In Christ Alone." Gettymusic.com. April 14, 2012. Retrieved April 24, 2018.

For the One:
"Reckless Love (Single) by Cory Asbury on Amazon Music—Amazon.com." Amazon.com. October 27, 2017. Retrieved January 22, 2018.

"Oh, Lord, My Rock and My Redeemer." Sovereign Grace Music. Prayers of the Saints (Live), 2017.

"Reckless Love (Single) by Cory Asbury on Amazon Music—Amazon. com." Amazon.com. October 27, 2017. Retrieved January 22, 2018.

ABOUT THE AUTHOR

 Morgan Cheek is a master's social worker, public speaker, and stay-at-home mom to Ally and Bailey Grace—two wonderfully, uniquely, and differently abled twin girls who have been diagnosed with a rare genetic mutation, HECW2. She resides in Birmingham, Alabama, with her husband, Hugh, who is a general pediatrician. At the time of this book's publication, Morgan and Hugh are in the process of bringing home their almost seven-year-old son from China. Cheek is the author of *On Milk and Honey: How God's Goodness Shows up in Unexpected Places*. She is also the writer at "His Hands, His Feet, His Heart," a blog with a focus on learning to see God in all things.

Made in the USA
Lexington, KY
10 June 2018